"It was with a fair measure of skepticism that I began reading this book, muttering to myself, 'Oh no, not another book on raising perfect kids!' But I was greatly surprised and gratified to see that this book was anything but. The Blackabys have shared their experiences from a two-generational perspective and I found their advice thoughtful, biblical and challenging. There are no cookie-cutter formulas in this book...thankfully! What I found instead was an approach to parenting that took each individual child into consideration and focused on character formation rather than compliance. I laughed and I cried as I vicariously shared their experiences, but I ended this book encouraged that there is a voice for parenting that is wise, full of grace, and just plain fun. Enjoy the book!"

Jim Keller
Licensed Mental Health Counselor, Founder and President,
Charis Counseling Center in Orlando, FL, Teaching Pastor,
Summit Church, Author, *The Upside-Down Marriage*

"Richard is a gifted storyteller. I always enjoy hearing him use real-life stories to explain and apply profound truths. Now it is clear that his daughter Carrie is a highly entertaining and insightful storyteller as well. You will thoroughly enjoy reading this book. It is filled with humor, insight, and godly wisdom. I highly recommend it to parents. It will leave you thinking, laughing, and changing and will result in a blessing for your children."

Dr. Henry T. Blackaby
Author, *Experiencing God*

"I enjoyed this book so much I decided to put my name on the manuscript and publish it first! Seriously, this book reminded me of the way Ramona and I raised our kids—not with perfection—but with purpose. Success was measured by faith, character, and a rollicking good time. We have seen it pay off. I know you will too."

Phil Callaway
Radio Host, Laugh Again,
Author, *Tricks My Dog Taught Me About Life, Love and God*

"This book was so much fun to read, I couldn't put it down! I felt like I was spending the afternoon with the Blackabys as they shared very real examples of 'rebellious parenting.' In this practical and biblically based book, Richard and his daughter Carrie have written a wonderful resource to help parents make good judgment calls, overcome the pressures of conventional wisdom to discern what is best for their child, and learn to enjoy the journey of parenting. They provide insights into raising children in a joyful setting that looks for 'opportunities to turn ordinary life experiences into happy memories.'"

Rhonda Stoppe
Author, *Moms Raising Sons to Be Men*

"Conventional wisdom isn't always wise or right or best. It's just familiar. One brief conversation with a Venezuelan-born doctor altered my cultural perspective and changed the course of my parenting when my three children were teens. After reading Richard and Carrie Blackaby's book, I wished I could turn back the clock and tweak a few more things! Give this book to every young family you love! Their children will thank you one day."

Connie Cavanaugh
International Speaker,
Author, *Following God One Yes at a Time*

"As a mom of six I started my parenting years with dreams of who I thought my kids should be, but that only led to frustration when they did not fit the mold my mind had created! As the years passed, God was faithful in showing me His unique designs and plans for each of my children.

"Richard and Carrie Blackaby share inspiring truths on parenting our children to thrive in Rebellious Parenting. In a society in which parents strive to keep up with 'conventional wisdom,' this father and daughter team speak to the heart of the matter. The Blackabys guide parents on how to put the pitfalls of popular opinion behind them and instead seek God's truth. God didn't create assembly lines, but rather one-of-a-kind humans. I love this book! It's inspiring, insightful, and filled with wisdom and truth. I can't wait to share it with friends, and read it again myself!"

Tricia Goyer
Author of 45 books, including *Lead Your Family Like Jesus, and Plain Faith: A True Story of Tragedy, Loss,* and *Leaving the Amish*

ReBELLiOUs
PARENTING

DARING TO BREAK THE RULES
SO YOUR CHILD CAN THRIVE

CARRIE BLACKABY &
RICHARD BLACKABY

Blackaby Ministries International
Jonesboro, GA

Editorial Work: AnnaMarie McHargue

Cover Design: Aaron Snethen

Layout Design: Aaron Snethen

Published by Blackaby Ministries International
P.O. Box 1035
Jonesboro, GA 30237
www.blackaby.org

ISBN (paperback): 978-1-7338536-1-3
ISBN (ebook): 978-1-7338536-2-0

Library of Congress Control Number: 2016942590

I'd like to dedicate this book to my parents, Henry and Marilynn, who did an awesome job, against some daunting challenges, of raising me into adulthood; and to my three children, Mike, Daniel, and Carrie, who overcame my parental shortcomings to become amazing adults.

— Richard Blackaby

I dedicate this book to my parents and to my incredible husband, Sam.

— Carrie Blackaby

Table of Contents

Preface

What does a rebel look like? An assortment of troubling images comes to mind.

Perhaps the most stereotypical protesters of the last century were the hippies from the 60s and 70s, with their long, grimy hair and fluorescent, tie-dyed clothing. They shunned materialism, proper hygiene, the "establishment," and the Vietnam War in favor of love, peace, and an ample supply of marijuana. Rebels of later years included punk rockers with their studded belts, pink Mohawks, and Chuck Taylor high-top shoes. They used distorted electric guitars and shouted vocals in adrenaline-fueled rants against authority figures, such as their washed-up fathers or the president of the United States.

Though their appearance, music, or causes may differ through the years, all rebels have one thing in common: They make a deliberate choice to defy socially accepted norms. We often assume we can identify rebels by their loud music or bizarre hairstyles. But a counterculture, by definition, is any movement that rejects the prevailing values, methods, or practices of society.

This book is our expression of rebellion against the "conventional wisdom" of today's parenting culture. We don't intend to write poetry or launch new fashion trends. We won't advocate a strike or pitch a tent in front of City Hall, but we will encourage you to rebel.

* * *

This book is unique for the Blackaby family of authors. While it is not the first father/daughter book to be written (Henry Blackaby did that with his daughter Carrie already), it is the first father/daughter book written about family.

In some ways, we are an unlikely duo to collaborate on a book. Yes, we share a bloodline, but that's where our physical similarities end. One of us is a middle-aged man waging a constant battle with nature to recede his middle faster than his hairline. The other is in her mid-20s and is less winded after running a half marathon than her dad is after fetching the mail. One of us grew up poor with the fashion sense of Mr. Rogers; the other was a princess with clothes so of-the-moment trendy, they went out of style before she could get them home from the store.

In other ways, we are strikingly similar. Both of us get incredibly cranky when we are hungry (we refer to Carrie's appetite as *The Beast*). Both of us love roller coasters (the higher, faster, and twistier, the better). We both tend to be task-driven, and we both value education. We were both brought up to be critical thinkers (in the analytical, not the judgmental sense), but we also learned to poke fun at ourselves and to enjoy the lighter side of life. You'll see this in some of the stories we tell.

* * *

If you've read other books written by members of our family, you may know that for many generations, the Blackaby family has enjoyed a rich Christian heritage. Our family tree is laden with ministers, godly businesspeople, and authors. Henry Blackaby wrote the popular study, *Experiencing God*, as well as many other influential books.

All five of Henry's children grew up to become Christian leaders. Richard is Henry's oldest son and has authored or co-authored dozens of books on numerous subjects, including leadership, Christian living, and life's seasons.

All three of Richard's children are now adults. Mike and Daniel are happily married to wonderful godly women (whose names, coincidentally, are both Sarah). Mike and Daniel have published a total of five books in the non-fiction and fantasy genres. Both of them serve in Christian ministry and have earned Ph.D.s in the fields of apologetics and Christianity and the Arts.

Carrie, the co-author of this book, is a fifth generation Blackaby author. She holds a Master of Fine Arts degree in creative nonfiction writing, as well as a Master of Theological Studies degree. She is married to a talented young man named Sam, and together they have a beautiful daughter named Claire.

I (Richard) am deeply thankful to God for my children and their spouses. When I speak in public, I often reference brilliant parenting techniques my wife, Lisa, used while rearing our children. Those who know her realize she is loaded with unusual insights into parenting and creating a joy-filled home. However, Lisa lunges for cover every time someone holds a microphone near her, so Carrie and I are thrilled that Lisa will put down in print, for the first time, her thoughts on family. Throughout t his b ook, s he'll m ake g uest appearances in the form of notes from "Mom."

We mention the current status of our family not to boast, since much of what we have was passed down to us, but to emphasize two things:

First, our family, though imperfect, is wholesome, God-following, and happy. Like you, we live in a society filled with struggling families. It is estimated that 70 percent of children who grow up regularly attending church with their family will leave their faith some time between high school and college graduation. Many homes are characterized by sadness and conflict rather than laughter. Our family discovered it didn't have to be that way. Second, though we come from a long line of respected Christian ancestors, our family chose not to live exactly the way they (or anyone else) did. Their methods weren't necessarily incorrect, but they would have been wrong for us. We realized that even a godly heritage needs tweaking from one generation to the next.

Don't assume that because we are writing a book on family we see ourselves as gurus who always get it right—far from it! You'll soon discover that we are extremely fallible people who are still finding our way as a family. But too many homes are struggling today for us to remain silent and withhold the wisdom we've uncovered with God's help. We hope you will be encouraged by our quirks, entertained by our missteps, and enlightened by our conclusions.

Richard and Carrie Blackaby

Chapter One

The Pitfalls of Popular Opinion
Rebelling Against Conventional Wisdom

"Beware of false knowledge. It is more dangerous
than ignorance."
—*George Bernard Shaw*

Ursula Trap

My (Carrie) first exposure to the film *The Little Mermaid* came
shortly after I turned five. It was perhaps the most traumatic event I'd
experienced up until that point (well, aside from the time my brother
Daniel crashed my princess birthday party dressed as Pocahontas).
The image of Ursula, with her slimy tentacles and garish makeup,
seared itself into my mind and haunted my dreams. I was young
and illiterate; my knowledge of villains was confined to the realm
of coloring books and Nickelodeon cartoons. But I was positively,
absolutely certain about one thing: *Ursula was coming for me.*

Living under the weight of my imminent demise was a burden
upon my preschool shoulders, so after weeks of nightmares and
sleepless nights, I decided to enlist the help of my older brothers.

"No problem!" Mike said. He patted me on the back. "We'll
help you lay a trap so she won't be able to sneak into your room at
night."

Mike headed the operation as lead engineer, and he, Daniel, and
I spent the evening constructing elaborate booby traps with Legos®.
My room became a veritable Fort Knox.

That night, for the first time in weeks, I didn't dread bedtime. My older and wiser siblings assured me of their extensive knowledge of underwater Disney villains. If anything could keep her out, it was our barricade. Secure in their promises, I snuggled against my pillow and my eyelids began to droop.

"Now remember," Mike said, perched at the foot of my bed, "these will definitely keep her out. If they're still in place when you wake up, you'll know she didn't come."

"We're just down the hall if you need us," Daniel added as he tucked the sheets under my chin. They wished me goodnight and left the room. I was asleep before the door closed behind them.

The next morning, the sunlight streamed in through my slatted blinds. I remembered the Ursula traps and opened my eyes. My stomach reeled as I glanced at the floor. All of the traps had been set off. The evidence led to a single inescapable conclusion.

Ursula had been there.

My nightmares returned. I became a five-year-old insomniac, staying awake until the wee hours, straining to discern the faint sound of tentacles slithering down the hallway toward my room.

Mike and Daniel still love to reminisce about "that time they set the Ursula traps off while Carrie was asleep."

Conventional Wisdom

Conventional wisdom is any generally accepted set of beliefs and practices. Its conclusions aren't necessarily followed because of their proven effectiveness, but simply because they are popular.

A common advertising gimmick uses the "ratio" ploy. The dreamy actor in a white lab coat declares, "Nine out of ten dentists recommend" this toothpaste, or that mouthwash. Or a fellow with a European accent says, "Four out of five gastrointestinal specialists regularly prescribe this laxative for regularity." But Carrie's experience taught her that you can't always trust the majority, or put another way, the majority isn't correct on every occasion in every circumstance.

This principle is no more evident than in the fashion industry. To cite a few examples:

- The misconception in the 80s that mullets were attractive. (Sorry, Billy Ray Cyrus.)

- The misconception in the 80s that shoulder pads the size of tea cozies were flattering.

- The misconception in the 80s that spandex neon bodysuits… well, you get the point.

- The current myth that jeans should dangle precariously midway down the wearer's thigh.

The health industry is also riddled with fluctuating "facts." Widely held conclusions based on scientific opinion are accepted by the masses, only to be amended later or even renounced. Coffee has gone from villain to hero more times than Severus Snape. Milk, once dubbed the perfect food, is now the "silent killer." We dread the day scientists change their view about the health benefits of dark chocolate.

Mom: Just because something is presented in an appealing package, that doesn't make it a good gift.

Clearly, just because practices or beliefs are popular today, doesn't mean they won't be tossed onto the scrap heap of outdated opinions tomorrow.

What You Don't Know Can Kill You

On December 13, 1799, the most famous American of his era mounted his horse and made his daily rounds on his large estate. Three inches of wet snow fell, drenching George Washington. That evening, he developed a sore throat. His wife, Martha, urged him to take medication, but he believed in letting illnesses run their course.

By the next morning, Washington suffered from chills and strep throat. Martha summoned their physician, Dr. Craik, but before he arrived, Washington's overseer, a man named Rawlins, entered the room and drew a knife. Despite Mrs. Washington's protests, Rawlins cut open the ailing general's arm so that blood began flowing. Washington ultimately died. Was it murder? Was it the first presidential cover-up? No. It was conventional wisdom.

The great general who had once quipped that there was "something charming" in the sound of musket balls being fired at him in battle was not a masochist. Medical practitioners of the time employed a procedure called bloodletting, which dated back to the scientific experiments of the ancient Greeks. Experts believed that some illnesses were caused by imbalances in the human body's four primary fluids, so removing "excess" blood

Mom: One of the quickest ways to lose your child's attention is to start a sentence with "When I was your age..."

8

could help restore a healthy inner equilibrium. Hence the practice of dropping leeches onto a patient's chest. As if being deathly ill were not disturbing enough.

By the late 1700s, medical advances had caused physicians to second-guess the value of bloodletting, but Washington still believed in it, so he instructed his assistant to initiate the process. When Dr. Craik arrived, he bled Washington for the second time. Eventually, two other medics came to help. The younger one, Dr. Elisha Dick, diagnosed Washington with a throat infection and recommended an immediate tracheotomy. His senior colleagues disagreed. Tracheotomies were too dangerous, they said. They proposed further bloodletting.

By the fourth round, the blood ran slowly. The brave general confessed, "Doctor, I die hard, but I am not afraid to go." His last words were, "'Tis well." He was 67.

If Washington's illness occurred today, modern medical knowledge may well have cured him. (By the same token, had he died, a modern Martha Washington would sue the socks off those doctors.) Even back then, one of the medics knew of a procedure that might have saved Washington's life, but the aging warrior general chose to stick with an outdated, dubious remedy.

So What's The Problem?

Parents have goals for their children. We want them to become happy, successful adults. Christian parents also hope their children will embrace faith in Christ and uphold Christian values.

But despite their best intentions, many parents realize their parenting method isn't working as well as they hoped. Instead of enjoying a home filled with laughter, their house is consumed with stress and dissention. Rather than growing up to become devout Christian adults, their children lose interest in their faith and stop attending church.

People regularly tell me (Richard) about the anguish they feel as parents:

Mom: Many parents know their kids could be doing better, but they aren't making the necessary adjustments in their parenting.

Jordan was a charming preschooler, yet by the third grade, he had lost his joy in learning and was becoming increasingly attention-seeking.

Jim and Susan are devout Christians who take their three children to church every week, yet the children constantly bicker and fight. Family outings and vacations have become unbearable.

As a child, Amy was a sweet Christian girl who went to church with her parents every week. But when she entered high school, Amy became distracted by boys and parties. Her parents were shocked at how readily she lost her faith and her virginity.

How can people who work so hard to be good parents end up experiencing such disappointments? There are many contributing factors, but we contend that one of the main reasons is this: Despite the fact that parents are achieving disheartening results, they are not seriously rethinking their practices or making the necessary adjustments so their children can thrive. Many parents are experiencing failure in their home, despite the fact that they love their children and are doing everything they know to do.

Lofty Goals, Humbling Reality

Most parents have high hopes for their children from the day they are born. Who knows what potential each bundle of humanity possesses? Could they be elected to government? Become doctors and heal the sick? Solve heinous crimes on the police force or teach the next generation in school? Moms and dads believe their child has the opportunity to accomplish more than they did (hence the obnoxious parents at Little League games).

I (Richard) was a typical, idealistic dad when Lisa and I carted our first child, Mike, off to kindergarten. So many decisions burdened my mind that day: When he graduated *summa cum laude* from high school, would we enroll him at Harvard or Yale? Should he attend a local university so we could more easily watch him quarterback his college football team to the national title?

Mom: "The best way to give advice to your children is to find out what they want and then advise them to do it."
— *Harry Truman*

Then we went to our first parent/teacher interview. The teacher described watching Mike squirm in his desk chair as if his pants were infested by a colony of fire ants.

Oh, well. Massachusetts has harsh winters anyway…

At least Daniel, our second born, knew how to sit still. He progressed nicely until First Grade "show and tell." That wasn't in Daniel's contract. So, our cherub became an escape artist, running away from school every time his teacher appeared less interesting than the Mario Kart Nintendo game waiting for him at home.

At least he is showing initiative, we rationalized…

Hope resurfaced when our daughter, Carrie, was born. She was our overachiever. I knew she wouldn't let me down. I wrote a form letter we could send to the colleges we would have to regretfully decline, despite the impressive, full-ride scholarships they were offering.…

Carrie's kindergarten teacher was a seasoned veteran. She made appointments the week before school started and visited the children in their homes to help alleviate any first-year jitters. To me, that seemed appropriate for other kids, but entirely unnecessary in Carrie's case. But, to set a good example for Carrie's classmates, we scheduled a home visit. Lisa arranged a child's tea table in Carrie's bedroom. A dish of dainties was tastefully laid out with child-appropriate beverages. Mrs. Wilson, a pleasant, motherly type, arrived on schedule and made her way to Carrie's room for some private time. We assumed she would probe Carrie's thoughts on the nation's abysmal educational record or perhaps ask her opinion on current trends among preschoolers.

Moments later, Carrie emerged from the room and abruptly closed the door behind her, leaving Mrs. Wilson to sip her tea in solitude. Carrie slumped dramatically against the closed door. "I just *had* to get out of that room!" she announced, rolling her eyes. "I could hardly *breathe!*"

Well, perhaps our grandchildren...

Like most parents, Lisa and I eventually adjusted our expectations to correspond with reality.

It's in the Bible

Today, if you mention the Bible in certain circles, you will be labeled an out-of-date traditionalist. Nevertheless, the Bible continues to be the most revolutionary book in print.

The apostle Paul was indoctrinated in the prevailing values and customs of his day. The most prestigious group in his nation was a political organization called the Sanhedrin. Paul aspired to enter into its esteemed ranks in record time. The most popular religious group was known as the Pharisees. Paul strove to outdo them in fervency. He zealously embraced his generation's trending values and wholly bought into his culture's measures of success.

Then he had a life-changing meeting with Christ. The encounter left him blind for three days (Acts 9:9). When the scales fell from his eyes, Paul saw his life accurately for the first time. He immediately cast aside his former customs and habits and began living the life God had always intended for him. Paul formerly embodied everything his society cherished, but Christ transformed him into a revolutionary.

Paul joined a movement so dynamic that 2,000 years later, we still experience its repercussions. Christianity turned popular views on marriage, child-rearing, and life in general upside down. One of the most profound pieces of advice Paul wrote was this:

"And do not be conformed to this world, but be transformed by the renewing of your mind, that you may prove what is that good and acceptable and perfect will of God." (Rom. 12:2)

After years of getting it wrong, Paul realized that you can't let mainstream society dictate your life; instead, you must embrace who God created you to be.

What's a Parent to Do?

Many parents know their children are struggling or could be doing better, but fail to act in ways that help their child succeed. We contend that one of the primary reasons for this is because modern society inundates families with misguided solutions to their problems.

In our frenzied culture, we can tap in to a steady stream of bite-sized phrases on social media. We simply scroll down and snatch up what appeals to us. There are potluck-styled sites that circulate inspirational quotes and maxims so everyone can partake. It's a motivational smorgasbord.

Mom: Sometimes we should doubt the benefits of giving others the benefit of the doubt.

However, just because an opinion is widely publicized doesn't make it wise or even true. Faulty thinking presented in a touching video or written in calligraphy and illustrated with rainbows is still faulty. It's up to us to discern between wisdom and fallacy. Here are a few examples of pithy quotes on social media right now:

Get lost finding yourself.
If you can dream it, you can do it.
Create your happy, whatever that means to you.
Trust your instinct.

Dream big.

The only failure is not trying.

Life is 10 percent inspiration and 90 percent perspiration.

It's easier now than ever before to let others do our thinking for us. Society brims with advice and opinions for how you should parent your child. Unfortunately, modern society is becoming increasingly intolerant of people who don't follow its politically correct approach. Ironically, in an age when advice is

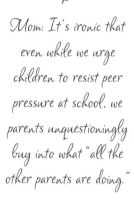

Mom: It's ironic that even while we urge children to resist peer pressure at school, we parents unquestioningly buy into what "all the other parents are doing."

more available than ever before, families continue to struggle. The challenge for parents is to discern what, if anything, in conventional wisdom is best for their child. It could be that what seems to be working for other children simply isn't the best option for everyone.

To Homeschool or Not to Homeschool

Partway through my seventh grade year, I (Carrie) had an epiphany: I didn't want to go to school anymore. Most children reach that conclusion at some point in their educational odyssey, and many do so a lot sooner than I did. My brother Daniel had tried to fix the problem by running home at recess in first grade. But, what can I say? I'm a late bloomer. I didn't want to quit school altogether—I wanted to try homeschooling.

When I mention that I was homeschooled, I often receive a sympathetic comment about my mother being unwilling to send me off to a "real" school. The implication is, "What child in her right mind would willingly agree to such a life of torture, isolation, and overall strangeness?" But the choice was entirely my own.

Mom: Just because a saying is written in calligraphy and posted on social media, that doesn't mean it's good advice.

The desire didn't stem from the usual presumed reasons. At the time, I was attending a private Christian school with dedicated, godly teachers. I wasn't being bullied, and I had a solid group of friends. I was a straight A student, and my teacher liked me. Aside from my frequent absences from gym class during the eight-week flag football unit because of my "hereditary weak ankles," everything was going well. I just felt that I was missing something.

I didn't know how my parents would react to such a radical change in my education, so I made a list of the pros and cons and presented it to them. I still have the list. It says:

Pros

- I can get more sleep.

- I won't have to miss youth group on Wednesday evenings to do homework.

- I can join book club with Olivia and Mya.

- I will have more time to figure skate. (Plus: I won't have to play flag football ever again in my life, ever.)

- I can work as fast or slowly as I need to.

- It sounds fun!

Cons

- I will miss my friend Hannah.

That afternoon, my parents and I sat down for a family business meeting in the living room. They'd never considered homeschooling me. After all, I was doing well and was the teacher's pet. Why fix what wasn't broken?

Mom, a free spirit, was intrigued by the prospect of being a homeschool mom (and not just so she could wear Amish-style clothing and grow herbs in window pots). Dad wasn't as open to the idea. He grew up in a family that believed in public school education. He admitted that his experience in junior high was miserable, but he had survived, so it didn't seem logical to him for his daughter to walk away from a great private school education. Nevertheless, by the end of our discussion, my parents agreed to give home education a try.

The next week I began my new life—and I loved it. I felt more rested. I rarely got sick. I had more time to participate in church activities. I joined a book club. I was able to practice my ice-skating more frequently, and I even went on field trips with other homeschoolers to museums and live theater events. My dad took me with him on business trips to exotic places, including England,

France, Singapore, Australia, New Zealand, and Malaysia. It was amazing!

But with my delight came something not so fun: misunderstanding. And criticism. Even some of my relatives and friends expressed concerns about my future. Didn't I want to go to college one day? Shouldn't I have a circle of friends that wasn't limited to my brothers and pet fish? Why did I never mention the horrific bullying I must have experienced at school to drive me to such a drastic "last resort"?

While many people supported my decision, I was stung by the insensitive comments of others. Eventually, I had to decide whether or not I was going to allow people's opinions to guide my life, or if I had the courage to follow through with what my parents and I knew was the best choice for me, regardless of how compelled others (including total strangers) felt to enlighten me.

> Mom: Why do we let total strangers tell us how to bring up our children? Why not listen to our kids?

I want to be clear: I'm not saying homeschooling is good and public schooling is bad. My oldest brother, Mike, never homeschooled a day in his life and he had a mostly positive experience. I also don't pretend that my experience homeschooling was without problems. But at the age of 12, I knew I was wired to homeschool, and if I let others sway me from that decision, I would be limiting myself from living my best life possible.

I ended up homeschooling through high school. I've since graduated from college with my Bachelor of Arts (*summa cum laude),* and hold two Master's degrees. Funny enough, now people rarely ask or care which educational method I used in high school.

We learned some unexpected lessons when we chose a different path than the one most people around us were taking. Interestingly, the great majority of critics we encountered had no firsthand knowledge of what they were advising us about. Though they had no experience with homeschooling, they had plenty of advice! Rather than asking us what we were learning, they'd offer, "I heard that…" Or, "I know someone who…" They were simply passing on myths or opinions they had picked up from secondary, often biased, sources. Too often, people heartily endorse (or dismiss) something without verifying their presuppositions. And that's what we are challenging.

Conclusion

It's important for parents to make decisions based on what is best for each individual child, not what the parents did when they were the same age, or what worked for other children.

Most parents already have a good idea what would work best for their children, but many don't know how to make it happen. Some admit that they lack the confidence to deviate from the status quo in certain areas of family life. Parents often

> *Mom: If you find yourself going in the wrong direction, it's better to redirect mid-way than continue on a course that is not taking you to where you want to go.*

19

assume they don't have the time or money to make their dreams or preferences a reality.

Criticism and misunderstanding are inevitable when you veer from what others do or believe. Enormous effort and sacrifice may be required. But at the end of the day, knowing you did what was best for your child is the supreme reward.

Reflect and Respond

1. What is one fallacy you used to believe? Perhaps it related to health, science, or relationships. How did you eventually realize you were mistaken in your belief?

2. Do you see yourself as a conformist or a rebel? Consider the following as you answer this question: If everyone you know is behaving in a certain way, do you tend to follow the majority's lead? How difficult is it for you to go against a societal norm and follow your personal convictions?

3. Consider your parenting philosophy. Are you confident you are following God's will for your family, or do you think there might be a better way than you are currently experiencing? Jot down two or three current practices or habits that you have questions about. These might not be evil or wrong in themselves, but maybe you suspect there is a better way. Then, review your list and ask God to guide you to His perspective.

4. At what age do you think children should have a say in their education? Why?

Action Ideas

1. If your parents are still living, ask them for their "top three" pieces of advice for families. Don't argue or challenge them. Just list them. Then compare how many of them you follow with your own family. What are the reasons for any discrepancies?

2. Do an Internet search on "good parenting practices" or "parental advice." Write down 10 that seem to be popular. Then evaluate how many of them you are practicing in your family. Consider why you are or are not following this popular advice.

3. Make a study of key passages in the Bible that talk about parenting. You might look through Proverbs, Deuteronomy 6:6-9, and Ephesians 6:1-4, as well as others. List the Biblical instructions to parents that you find. Compare your list with modern views on parenting.

4. Go for coffee with a friend or friends. Ask them what their views on parenting are. Don't argue or debate them! Just list them. Then reflect on how much your parenting is like or unlike that of your friends.

5. Peruse a bookstore's section on family. Examine the various titles. Look at the summary on the back of the book covers. What do you surmise about popular teaching on parenting today? How does that line up with what you have been doing?

Chapter Two

Land of the Free, Home of the Clones

Rebelling Against Conformity

"Today you are you! That is truer than true! There is no one alive who is you-er than you!"
—Dr. Seuss

Blue Hair and a Near-Death Experience

I (Richard) was the president of a theological seminary in Canada for 13 years. During my tenure, all three of my children became teenagers.

One year, our church made a directory that required every family to be photographed. That's when I had a brilliant idea for a public relations masterstroke. Every Christmas, I received exquisite photographs of other school presidents with their attractive families. They had heartwarming captions like, "In this season of glad tidings, my family and I would like to wish you and yours…" It was high time our donors and alumni received a Christmas picture of my good-looking family!

On the day of our scheduled appointment, I arrived home from the office and bellowed, "All right, everybody, time to go! Our photo shoot is in less than thirty minutes!"

Always punctual, Lisa emerged from our bedroom. She looked beautiful.

I love to see a great plan come together!

Another minute, and my daughter, Carrie, burst out of the upstairs bathroom and sashayed down the stairs sporting the latest in fashion with her customary flair.

A vision of teenage loveliness.

Next, my 16-year-old son Daniel appeared. He wore a knitted cap and a baggy hoodie. His outfit was entirely appropriate, if he intended to hold up a convenience store. But before I could ask if disturbing band logos could be Photoshopped out, I caught sight of Mike standing in the entryway. There stood my oldest child with his hair spiked like a porcupine and the tips dyed *fluorescent blue*.

"Hi, Dad!" he hollered. "I'm your son, and I have blue hair!"

"Yes, and *both* those facts deeply disturb me at this moment," I muttered.

Terms like *respectability*, *reputation*, and *ridiculous* whirled around my brain in a vortex. I opened my mouth to spew them, but had only proceeded as far as, "*What, in the name of all that is good and decent…*" when I felt a hand on my arm. It was Lisa. She whispered, "*Temporary hair dye.*" I got the point.

At the moment, my beloved boys looked as sophisticated as the Marx brothers. Daniel based his wardrobe entirely on comfort and "coolness." I got that. But I didn't understand why Mike would spend money—probably mine—on Grover-blue hair dye and sculpt his locks into gravity-defying 3D structures. Mike was simply experimenting with his identity. He wanted to stand out from the crowd. I would have preferred he make his statement by having the highest GPA in his class, or ending hunger in Zimbabwe. But I guess he thought a tube of hair dye involved less commitment.

I didn't know it then, but Mike would go on to obtain a college education, a Master's degree in seminary, and a Ph.D. in apologetics. To date, he has two published books and is planting a church in Victoria, Canada. And I was ready to chew him out for being different. What was I thinking?

The reality was that all three of my children were unique individuals. Carrie was, and still is, a fashion diva who looks great every time she leaves the house. Daniel was our laid-back child who valued comfort over style. Mike was our wannabe rock star who liked to stand out from the crowd. All three were being true to their identity and values. What upset me was that they were not dressing in conformity with mine. But really, why would I want my kids to look and act just like everyone else—or like me, for that matter? And what made me think I could parent each child in exactly the same manner?

So What's the Problem?

God loves diversity. It's the hallmark of creation. The popular analogy claims no two snowflakes are identical. With the exception of Greenland (and Carrie's birth city of Winnipeg, Manitoba), snowflakes usually don't stick around long enough for anyone to verify that claim. So we'll talk about bugs instead.

If you were forming the world, how many insects would you include in your grand design? According to the Smithsonian Encyclopedia, more than 900 thousand different species of insects inhabit the planet today—and those are just the ones that have been documented. For example, the *Triatominae* group of insects (also known as "conenose" or "kissing" bugs) is a subfamily containing approximately 130 different species. They survive by sucking the blood from the lips of sleeping human beings. And here's a disturbing fact: they are common in the southern United States.

Another fascinating bug is the Japanese giant hornet. Fully grown, it can be several inches long with a sting that is said to be among the most painful of any insect. Its venom, which dissolves human tissue, can be lethal.

Researchers discover new species every year, and scientists consider current lists far from exhaustive. God put an enormous amount of creativity into a part of creation many people would be happy to see become extinct!

Indeed, God's ingenuity is apparent everywhere, especially in the human body, which is astounding in its complexity. For instance, over 2 million working parts operate in a single eyeball. In one second, your eye can focus on 50 different things, and in one hour, it can process up to 36,000 pieces of information. Fingerprints are commonly recognized as unique flags of our identity, but even our lips, tongues, and feet have one-of-a-kind markings. Science tells us that an adult human body is composed of about 7,000,000,000,0 00,000,000,000,000 atoms. God orchestrates an enormously complex production when He creates each individual!

Parents know that each of their children is unlike any other. Nevertheless, society demands that we squeeze them all into one preset mold. Compounding the problem are parents who take a one-size-fits-all approach to rearing their children.

It's in the Bible

The Bible reveals that God has created, called, and commissioned a wide array of one-of-a-kind human beings. Consider these examples:

- David was always an adventurous boy. He put Tom Sawyer to shame! Fighting lions and bears while tending his father's sheep might have raised a few eyebrows, but not even his father imagined his son would one day become his nation's most glorious king.

- Most children imagine epic scenarios where they save the day. Imagine Joseph's father's surprise when his son's boyhood dreams of rescuing his family and countrymen became a reality.

- Parents want their daughters to grow up chaste and wholesome. Imagine Mary's parents' reaction when they discovered their teenage daughter was pregnant before her wedding.

- Children love to pretend they are superheroes. Imagine what Samson's parents thought when he grew stronger than their ox!

One thing is clear: God delights in developing and working through a wide variety of people. We shouldn't be surprised that not all children are the same or need standard parenting. While God intends for everyone to become like Christ, He doesn't intend for them to be exactly like one another. Children have different personalities, experiences, and callings. That requires different parenting.

What's a Parent to Do?

Mike was our firstborn. He was generally a compliant, good-natured child, though the only way to get him to sit still was by firmly setting him in fresh concrete. He was a born party animal who was always smiling and never met a stranger he didn't take to immediately. Then came Daniel. He was quieter than his brother and more sedentary. He also had a huge stubborn streak. That little character trait became evident within the first few months when he would stiffen his body in an upside down "U" shape that we dubbed "the macaroni" and scream until his needs were met. We finally seemed to be getting a handle on our children's personalities. Then we had our dainty little girl, Carrie. Her brothers doted on her. Lisa and I (Richard) doted on her. In fact, everyone doted on her. We suppose that is how she developed into a princess.

Mom: Why do we encourage our children to "have the courage to be themselves" and then have a kissy fit if they dye their hair or wear clothes we don't care for?

As a family, we discovered something that parents with more than one child have been learning for centuries: Every child is different. Parenting would be so much easier if all children were identical! But because they are not, we had to first understand how God had uniquely "wired" each of our three children, and secondly, we had to adjust our parenting to match each child God gave us.

Children enter the world with an innate sense of freedom and imagination. They believe anything is possible. They have no inhibitions about trying new things and discovering what works. Unfortunately, around the time children enter school, their inquisitive confidence runs headlong into dream-defying reality in the classroom. This is due in part because, though it may be okay to "be yourself" at home, as soon as you go out into the world, you have to be concerned with your image.

Crazy Inside, Coiffured Outside

When I (Carrie) was a child, I loved to style my mom's hair. Mom would sit down in a chair and doze off while I attached every hair bow and ribbon I owned (enough to supply four seasons of *Toddlers in Tiaras*) at random places on her head. The feathery barrettes were my favorites, so I usually put those in the front.

Mom would inevitably gasp with delight when she looked in the mirror while I beamed with pride at my styling finesse. I could have taught Nick Arrojo a thing or two about updos. One day, when Mom was going to run some errands, I took extra care to position the barrettes and feathers "just so."

"Everyone will stop and say, 'Look at the gorgeous lady!'" I exclaimed as I admired my creation, bloated with pride. She dutifully said goodbye, got in the car, and drove away. I knew my mother would be the most elegant woman in the cereal aisle!

What I didn't know was that as soon as my longsuffering mother got into the car in the garage, she would painstakingly remove all of her hair apparel. Upon her return home, she would carefully reinstall my handiwork before re-emerging into the house to spare my feelings. On this particular day, Mom stopped at the bank, the grocery store, and the dry cleaners. When she pulled into our garage, she began to hurriedly replace the multitude of hairpieces before re-entering the house.

As she started pinning them back in, she felt something in her hair that was fluffy…feather-like, even…then she understood why every person she had encountered had grinned so widely at her. Horror of all horrors—her hair looked like the aviary at the San Diego Zoo, complete with plumage. After that incident, Mom began redirecting my fledgling creative efforts into less potentially embarrassing enterprises, like baking cookies. I didn't realize it at the time, but our "anything goes" attitude at home was being severely curtailed by concern for the opinions of people outside our house.

It's one thing to be innovative and daring at home.[1] But in public, we tend to form ranks and trudge in line with everyone else. We are inhibited by people's opinion far more than we like to admit. Our culture relentlessly pressures children, and their parents, to conform. Schools herd children through standardized tests, routines, and educational formulas. Companies follow bureaucratic policies and procedures. Clever marketing campaigns compel parents to make sure their child does what all the other kids are doing and has what all the other kids have.

> Mom: There is something immensely refreshing about off-the-wall people.

1 One time my brother Daniel broke out into dance to the Elvis song "All Shook Up" by himself in his room while wearing nothing but his boxers and a knitted hat. Only when he stopped to catch his breath did he notice that the blinds were open and he was in full view of our entire cul-de-sac. Our neighbors became intimately acquainted with his daring and creative side.

The end result is middle-aged adults who have long since sacrificed their youthful dreams on the altar of orthodoxy. People whose imaginations were overactive as children now march in sync to society's drumbeat.

School can be harsh on children who are "different." Society has a way of chipping away at our children's individuality and creativity until they look and act like everyone else. Parents can inadvertently compound the problem by treating all of their children exactly the same. "Why can't you be like your brother/sister?" has haunted many a child into adulthood. If you are going to encourage your children to identify, embrace, and celebrate their uniqueness, it won't be easy. You can expect plenty of teasing, trials, and tears. But it will be worth it! If you want to help your children develop their unique God-given personalities, here are three simple guidelines:

1. Encourage your children to express their individuality.

I (Carrie) have a spunky little cousin named Madi. She recently started kindergarten at a school that requires uniforms. On the first day of school, her mom dressed her in the school-issued navy-blue skirt and red blouse. Madi looked in the mirror and frowned.

"Mama," she said. "This is not my style. I look like a boy."

Mama: "But you're wearing a skirt."

Madi: "It's not pink; it's blue, Mama."

Mama: "It's the rules, Madi."

Madi: "I am having a hard time with all these rules, Mama."

A sympathetic adult warned Madi's mom that sending her to a school with a mandatory dress code would rob Madi of her individuality. Madi's mom replied, "The school may conform to Madi, but Madi will not conform to the school!"

Sure enough, Madi's "first day of school" photo shows her obediently wearing her uniform, along with a denim jacket, bright blue eyeglasses, purple backpack, yellow socks, multi-colored sandals, and a crisp white hair bow. We are cheering for young Madi as she strives to maintain her identity and self-respect in a world that is hard on non-conformists.

2. Help your children explore their options.

It's ironic that in the United States, where people pride themselves on their freedom, trends are, well, such a trend. Young people often resort to the "herd" mentality. They dress in the same clothes, listen to the same music, go to the same movies, and adopt the same vernacular. Parents reinforce this tendency by enrolling their children in the same lessons, sports, and educational activities as everyone else. We want our children to develop as individuals, but we often treat them as if they are not unique.

One way to help your children embrace their unique passions and gifts is by helping them explore the numerous options available to them. Someone who could be the poster child for this truth is another one of Carrie's cousins, Morgan.

Morgan: Breaking the Mold

I (Carrie) love spending time with my cousin Morgan, who is three years younger than I am. I don't think she has experienced a humdrum (or normal) moment in her life.

She loves to try extreme sports. So, quite predictably, she's broken several bones, some of them more than once. She recently injured her leg in a "freak" accident when she decided to walk around her house for a few days solely in a handstand position, just to change things up.

During her senior year in high school, Morgan got tired of sitting at a desk all day, so rather than the usual curriculum, she enrolled in an outdoor wilderness program. This was not an extended field trip for wimps. It was the kind where they dropped you off—Bear Grylls style—with nothing but a compass and a jackknife, and you had to use survival skills to get back to base camp. To complicate matters, it was February in Saskatchewan, Canada. Temperatures of 20 degrees below zero and three inches of snow didn't stop her from finding her way back to civilization—more specifically, to the nearest shopping mall.

Cousin Morgan loves fashion, food, books, driving a quad, snowboarding, playing the guitar, climbing up things, jumping off things, rappelling down things, and making artistic creations. To pay her way through college, Morgan is presently a fruit sculptor at a trendy local brunch bistro. She can make a watermelon look like a rose. She also does stints as the mascot at local sporting events. When she's not creating edible art, she is working with children in Mexico or taking surfing lessons in Hawaii. She recently returned from a 40-day whirlwind tour of 19 countries in Europe, which she paid for through her various unusual jobs.

Morgan's family moved to a different city when she was entering her senior year of high school. For most of us, that would be traumatic. Not for her. She walked into the cafeteria on the first day and announced, "I'm new here. Anyone else new too?" She had an instant circle of friends. Morgan inspires me to try new things and to laugh at myself.

3. Equip your child to go for it!

The only thing worse than not knowing what to do with your life is to know but lack the courage or the resources to go for it. It's common today for parents to praise their children for being one-of-a-kind. There are books, poems, and bumper stickers galore expressing the benefits of chasing your dream. But all that rhetoric is meaningless if parents aren't willing to help their children make those dreams a reality.

When Mike and Daniel were in their early teens, they wanted to form a rock band with their two best friends (another set of brothers) and become famous. I (Richard) knew that eventually they would probably choose other careers—at least I hoped they would. Still, I admired them for being visionaries. Lisa and I bought them a drum set and a guitar. We found a music school and drove them to and from lessons. We replaced broken drumsticks and lost guitar picks. We also bought ample supplies of earplugs so we were prepared for their practice sessions.

They poured themselves into their band. It was called Val Veeda (the name was loosely based on a cheese brand). They practiced loudly for hours in our basement. One thing led to another, and ultimately, they formed a new band with a more sophisticated sound (and a female vocalist who could actually sing).

The new band was called Fading Rebel. Their signature song was entitled "Strength to Stand," and was about having the courage to stand up for your faith. The band even toured for a while in neighboring cities with some better-known bands and played in some pretty sketchy venues. They made a CD and printed t-shirts with their logo emblazoned on them.

I recall attending one of the boys' performances. I was the president of a theological seminary at the time and a (somewhat) respected Christian leader in our community. I assumed I had a certain image to uphold. But there on stage were my two teenage boys. Both had hair that was way past due for a visit to the hair salon. Both sported piercings. Both were jumping all over the stage, head-banging, and doing acrobatic leaps off their amps. There were other adults from our church in attendance. I admit that I began to worry about what they would think (or tell others) about my children's behavior. Surely the teenage sons of a Christian author and speaker like myself should be occupying themselves ministering to the homeless or studying the Bible in the original Hebrew and Greek.

As I began to worry that perhaps I had been a bit too lenient in the standards I had enforced in our home, I suddenly felt a frantic tap on my arm. It was Lisa. She informed me that the crowd needed to get more involved in the music. And, as she often did on such occasions, she had a plan.

"Richard, get all the adults we know to join us, and let's charge the stage and start a mosh pit!" Gulp. Now my dear wife has had some pretty "out there" ideas before (like suggesting I quit my job and move our family to a small northern town where we could run a coffee shop and sell homemade snacks and crafts), but this was really pushing my envelope! The next thing I knew, I was timidly running up to the stage, jumping up and down and waving my hands. I had no idea what proper moshing etiquette involved.

What happened next surprised the life out of me. Teenagers from all over the auditorium spied the awkward, middle-aged adults pathetically trying to mosh to the music. Suddenly, the young people eagerly raced to join the fogies. Teenagers were hurling themselves against me, laughing, and urging me not to quit. I have thanked God every day since that no one caught that spectacle on camera. The next day, I was in so much pain I could barely crawl out of bed. But do you know what? Our kids couldn't believe it. They knew we supported them, but to launch a mosh pit that left people in our town still buzzing days later? That was epic!

Eventually, our boys outgrew their fixation with stardom. Now they both play regularly on the worship band at church. Are they rock stars? No. But they wouldn't trade the experience for anything. They learned much more than how to play an instrument. They made some terrific memories while they pursued their dreams. They also have a great deal on a t-shirt if you're interested...

It's not enough to spout motivational platitudes to your children about chasing their dream. They need you to do more than sit in your armchair and cheer them on. They need you to support them in visible ways: with your time, presence, and money.

The Cost of Following the Formula

My (Carrie) childhood friend Lacey was mercilessly bullied at school. She wanted to transfer to another school where many of her church friends were enrolled, or perhaps attend a Christian institution. Most of all, she longed to try homeschooling. While sympathetic, her parents told her she had to press on because 1) there was no bus service to the other school, 2) they couldn't afford private school, 3) her siblings were doing fine in the same circumstances, and 4) her mom didn't want to be tied down at home now that her children were school-aged.

So Lacey, a compliant child, trudged off to a school she despised. She often expressed resentment that her family didn't take her concerns seriously. Her school experience was miserable. She finally graduated and couldn't leave home fast enough. Free at last, she launched into a lifestyle that summarily rejected her parents' Christian beliefs and values.

Lacey's parents realized their daughter was struggling, but they failed to make the necessary modifications to their parenting practices so she could succeed. They felt bound to the only model of parenting they knew. Unfortunately, that model contributed to their daughter's downfall.

> Mom: If children never see their parents challenge prevailing customs, then they also may be ill-equipped to do so.

Challenge

For as long as I can remember, my (Carrie) parents encouraged my brothers and me to seek God's direction for our lives. I grew up knowing that our best interests were not always achieved by following the lead of our friends. We also learned that mimicking what our parents had done at our age wouldn't necessarily be right for us either (not to mention, my dad's scraggly, lopsided 70s afro is

> *Mom: Parenting is tough. But the good news is, we can learn from each other's successes and mistakes.*

a little difficult to replicate). Though we made some mistakes along the way, each of us developed a unique life that, so far, has been extremely rewarding.

A few years ago for Christmas, my mom bought me a t-shirt bearing a quote from my favorite author, Mark Twain (who was many things, but certainly not a conformist). It says, "Whenever you find yourself on the side of the majority, it is time to pause and reflect." That statement sums up my family's motto.

Conclusion

When people settle for bland, uninspired living, they insult their Creator. It is your responsibility as a parent to help your children understand the multi-dimensional individual God created them to be. Don't allow the world, society, your children's friends, or your own parenting to diminish their God-given uniqueness. At the end of the day, don't worry if your kids don't turn out exactly as you hoped. You certainly need not be alarmed if they grow up to be different than their friends. Rather, do all you can to ensure that each of your children has the courage, support, and tenacity to blossom into the person they were meant to be.

Reflect and Respond

1. What is an example of the way you celebrate your child's individuality? How might you have inadvertently suppressed your child's unique spirit and characteristics in your effort to help them fit in?

2. Do you have the nerve to allow your children to take a different path than the one their friends are choosing? Are you prepared for the inevitable comments you may receive from other adults?

3. Jot down the most recent thing you did in your family that would be considered non-traditional. What happened? Would you do it again? Why or why not?

4. Do you praise your children for their uniqueness and individual successes? In praising one child, have you inadvertently made one of your other children feel inadequate by comparison?

Action Ideas

1. Write the names of each of your children on a separate page. List the unique qualities (good or not so good) about each one. Then list unique ways you are parenting them to accommodate for their individuality. List anything you might need to start doing that might help each particular child to thrive.

2. Make a lunch date with each of your children. Ask them how they see themselves as unique from their siblings and from their friends. If they have difficulty identifying anything, brainstorm with them. Then ask how they feel they might need to be parented differently in light of their individual personality.

3. Go shopping and find a poster or humorous item that celebrates a particular characteristic of each child. Perhaps have a special family meal where you present the gifts and celebrate the uniqueness of each family member.

4. Have a family meeting about your family's "culture." Discuss how your family is different from other families. Don't let this be a time to criticize other families, but instead, to consider your own family's uniqueness. Brainstorm ways you might do certain activities that would be unique to your family. Talk openly about the fact that you are willing to develop a family that is different from other families in positive ways.

Chapter Three

Look Around You...Stupid Is Everywhere!
Rebelling Against Stupidity

"We shall require a substantially new manner of thinking if mankind is to survive."
—*Albert Einstein*

Stupid at 30,000 Feet

When I (Carrie) was 10 years old, our family planned a trip to Disney World. I was euphoric—what kid doesn't dream of visiting Mickey? We lived in Canada, the land of perpetual winter, so the excitement of spending a week in the sunshine state was almost unbearable.

The flying time from Calgary to Orlando was six hours. For an adult, that's a pretty long flight. For a kid, travel time is magnified in direct proportion to the allure of the destination, which made that particular trip roughly seventeen eternities.

My brothers and I settled into our row near the front of the plane, fidgeting and fighting over which one of us got the window seat. This was just a formality, since we already knew how the fight would end. Mike always won because he was the biggest. As the youngest and weakest, I ended up squashed in the middle seat. I tried to cram my carry-on under the seat, but it didn't fit.

"Give me your backpack," Mike said, trying to make some room underneath the seat in front of him. Reaching down, he latched on to an object and tried to move it out of the way. "Hey, this thing won't budge." He tugged at it, twisting back and forth.

Suddenly, the object kicked. Apparently, the man in front of us wanted his foot back.

Mom had advised us to pack plenty of activities to keep us busy: games, books, that sort of thing. We ran out of stuff to do by the time the flight attendants finished the seatbelt demonstration. Mike dozed off. Daniel and I passed some time obnoxiously changing each other's in-flight radios to the classical music station, but the novelty of that quickly wore off. The movie commenced—it was boring. We ate all the snacks Mom had packed. Finally, we had nothing left to do but to stare aimlessly ahead as we slowly lost our sanity.

I was cold, so I reached up and twisted the air vent closed. Daniel reached up and twisted it open.

I reached up to close it again, glaring at him.

He slapped my hand away and reopened it. I retaliated in similar fashion and closed it.

He stood and opened it. I stood and closed it.

The dispute continued, mounting in intensity. It was no longer about the air temperature. It became a conflict of wills so epic it made the Battle of Thermopylae look like a playground tussle between first graders.

We fought on the beaches. We battled in the air, on the landing grounds, in the fields, streets, and hills...

I was about to rally the troops and launch a final assault when a loud noise distracted me. It came from the woman in the seat directly behind me. "AHEM!!!" She was glaring at us.

In fact, several passengers were staring at us. Apparently, our little skirmish was not as entertaining to them as it was to us, especially since our air vent was located directly in front of the movie screen.

We had no idea so many people were watching our childish antics. But, of course, the foolish choices we make can, and often do, directly impact other people. I remember my parents frequently pointing out to my brothers and me that "stupid is everywhere."

So What's the Problem?

This is the age of political correctness. Self-appointed watchdogs are constantly on the lookout for bigots who might disparage someone else's behavior or choices. Anyone who has the courage to call immorality what it actually is—sin—is slapped with the label intolerant faster than you can say "double standard." A husband is constantly making humiliating, chauvinistic comments in public to his wife, but who are we to judge? If she is okay with it, then it's no one else's business. A teenage girl at church dresses provocatively, but that's her business, not ours. Ours is not to judge, right?

Mom: We should do our kids a favor and teach them early how to recognize stupidity.

If there's anything modern society won't tolerate, it's intolerance. Parents teach their kids how to cross the street safely and how to drive defensively. Adults admonish youngsters not to play with matches and warn them to refrain from talking to strangers. They keep toxic chemicals and medicine out of reach and make sure their children wear helmets while riding their bikes. Moms and dads threaten dire punishment if a child is caught smoking or shoplifting. But, for fear of sounding judgmental, many parents don't point out equally dangerous behavior that has even greater destructive potential.

Some families don't allow the word stupid to be used in their home. Indeed, numerous euphemisms exist, including imprudent, ill-advised, thoughtless, injudicious, and so on. Parents of small children may prefer a gentler term, such as silly. That's fine, but in our family we reserved the word stupid for the selfish, rude, rash, and dangerous behavior we wanted our children to avoid.

Silly is making funny faces or telling knock-knock jokes.

Stupid is bullying another child, or calling him names, or teasing her about a disability.

Silly is driving your children crazy with lame puns (Richard's forte).

Stupid is driving too fast. Or driving while intoxicated. Or getting intoxicated in the first place.

In their effort to avoid sounding critical, parents may excuse or simply ignore unacceptable behavior displayed by others, particularly by other adults. But, could it be that in our quest to be non-judgmental, we affirm the very destructive attitudes and habits that we want our children to avoid?

Mom: The Bible doesn't sugarcoat foolishness, and neither should we.

We're not suggesting that people should be labeled as stupid, but even highly intelligent beings can do stupid things (Albert Einstein did some doozies). The truth is, all of us are capable of foolish behavior. We aren't doing our children any favors by ignoring that fact.

It's in the Bible

The Bible talks a great deal about stupidity (often referred to as "folly") by repeatedly contrasting foolishness with wisdom. The book of Proverbs in particular wades in deep on the subject:

Fools despise wisdom and instruction. Proverbs 1:7

...fools hate knowledge. Proverbs 1:22

The complacency of fools will destroy them. Proverbs 1:32

A foolish woman is clamorous. She is simple, and knows nothing. Proverbs 9:13

...a foolish son is a grief to his mother. Proverbs 10:1

A prating fool will fall. Proverbs 10:10

The mouth of the foolish is near destruction. Proverbs 10:14

And the fool will be servant to the wise of heart. Proverbs 11:29

He who hates correction is stupid. Proverbs 12:1

The way of a fool is right in his own eyes. Proverbs 12:15

The heart of fools proclaims foolishness. Proverbs 12:23

A fool lays open his folly. Proverbs 13:16

The companion of fools will be destroyed. Proverbs 13:20

The wise woman builds her house, but the foolish pulls it down with her hands. Proverbs 14:1

A fool rages and is self-confident. Proverbs 14:16

What is in the heart of fools is made known. Proverbs 14:34

The lips of the wise disperse knowledge, but the heart of the fool does not do so. Proverbs 15:7

Excellent speech is not becoming to a fool. Proverbs 17:7

A foolish son is a grief to his father. Proverbs 17:25

A fool's mouth is his destruction. Proverbs 18:7

The Bible doesn't mince words when it comes to foolish actions. Neither should we.

What's a Parent to Do?

Every person on Earth is capable of foolish thoughts, decisions, words, and behavior. We've all heard from encouraging teachers or consultants, "There's no such thing as a dumb question." But we all know, as they do, that their maxim isn't always true. There are not only unwise questions, but also unwise answers. (If you don't believe us, watch a Miss America pageant.)

Kids need to know what stupid looks like, so they can avoid it.

1. Stupid uses flawed thinking.

The world is filled with opinions and behaviors that don't pass the common sense test. Parents need to teach their children how to recognize flawed thinking as soon as possible. Here are a few examples:

Christian parents allow their daughter to date a non-Christian young man, but not "get serious" unless he first becomes a Christian. Wrong! If you teach your daughter not to marry a non-Christian, why on earth would you let her date one? Only foolish parents allow their child to play with fire. The vast majority of the time, Christians who marry unbelievers date them first!

"We just look away during the sex scenes!" That's what some families say to justify watching movies with

Mom: Dangerous, foolhardy behavior ought to be regularly identified so no one in your home (including Mom or Dad) is tempted by it.

graphic depictions of sex, violence, language, or nudity. They explain, "It has a great story! It just has a couple of bad scenes in it." Our family had some great discussions on this topic. We concluded that you are still watching a movie that does not cut the muster of Philippians 4:8, even if you occasionally look away. And, you are still watching a film containing sexual and violent themes even if you don't watch during the most explicit scenes. It is crazy to believe such storylines are harmless simply because you avert your eyes before the characters take all of their clothes off. We also concluded that it would be hypocritical for us to claim to uphold Christian morals and then immerse ourselves in films that flaunted ungodly themes. Far better to find an activity that would not require us to rationalize our participation afterward.

As an aside, much of the "stupid thinking" our family grappled with was not promoted by non-Christians. Often, it was practices endorsed by members of our church. We never intended to become a holier-than-thou family. But neither did we want to accept bad thinking by those around us just because we were afraid of appearing judgmental. Our discussions generally occurred at home as we worked out our own beliefs. We didn't find it productive to argue or debate with other families about their practices.

2. Stupid is manipulative.

I (Carrie) found myself at a crossroads when I started third grade. Our small town was growing rapidly, and that year my grade was split into two classes to accommodate the influx of students. To my dismay, my best friend Rebecca and I ended up in opposite classes.

I was a shy kid, so the prospect of finding myself in a classroom full of strangers was as appealing as being chased by a pack of rabid dogs.

I was relieved on the first day of school when the girl assigned to the desk next to mine, Kristen, invited me to play with her at recess. Every recess Kristen and her group of friends played "Pony Pals,"[2] a game that involved galloping around the school playground neighing. I wasn't a huge fan of horses, but pretending to be one was better than playing alone. So I brushed up on my horse terminology and joined them.

Mom: If we want our children to avoid being manipulated, we have to teach them what manipulation looks like.

At first I had fun, but I soon discovered Kristen had a lot of rules for girls who wanted to be Pony Pals. For one, we had to play Pony Pals every recess (and play the way she wanted). Second, we could *only* play with other Pony Pals. I didn't like how demanding Kristen was, but none of the other girls seemed to mind. So every day I continued to trot around the playground with the Pony Pals.

One day, my mom suggested I invite my new friends over to our house to play. She bought cookie mixes, bright colored icing, and sprinkles for decoration. While we chatted and baked in the kitchen, my mom puttered around nearby. I later learned that she had noticed something disturbing in my behavior and wanted a chance to meet the girls I'd been spending time with.

---

2 Based on the book series *The Pony Pals*, which was extremely popular at the time.

As she listened, she was horrified by what she heard. The entire time we were baking, Kristen and the Pony Pals gossiped, criticized other girls in our class, and obsessed over boys. One of the Pony Pals had a birthday coming up, and Kristen told her which classmates she shouldn't invite to her party.

After they left, my mom and I chatted as we cleaned up the kitchen. She explained that people who say mean things about classmates and who get mad when their friends play with other people aren't acting like true friends.

The next day at recess I told Kristen I didn't want to be a Pony Pal anymore. Even though the next few weeks of school were difficult, I eventually made friends with other girls who weren't so demanding.

By teaching me to recognize and address manipulative behavior when I was young, my mom helped me avoid a lot of trouble and heartbreak as I got older. Where is the best place for kids to learn discernment? Not at school. Not on the playground. Not on the job. Not even at church. It's at home. Parents are the ones best equipped to help their children learn the delicate balance between cynicism and naiveté.

The goal parents are striving for with their children is found in the wise words of Christ as He sent His disciples into the world.

Mom: They say it takes a village to raise a child, but if parents aren't paying attention, a village can also ruin their child.

We want them to be "as shrewd as snakes and as innocent as doves." (Matthew 10:16)

3. Stupid is shortsighted.

Foolishness does not consider the consequences of poor decisions. Case in point: Nathan Wayne Pugh, 49, of Sachse, Texas, approached a teller at a Wells Fargo Bank and told her he was robbing the bank. While setting off the silent alarm, the courageous clerk informed Mr. Pugh that it was company policy not to release cash to anyone unless he first produced two pieces of ID. The dimwitted robber complied, including handing over his bankcard for that branch. The cashier jotted down the information and surrendered the funds. The police arrested Pugh as he exited the building.

Unfortunately, foolish behavior is common. We knew a teenager who was the star quarterback of his high school football team and a popular student. Drafted by a major college football program, his future sparkled with possibilities. But, with his growing popularity, the youth became increasingly attracted to the party scene. He began to drink heavily and experiment with drugs. Late night parties took their toll as he neglected his studies and abused his health. An injury ended his promising career. He plunged into a destructive spiral of drugs and alcohol that ultimately led to his expulsion from school. A life latent with potential was pitifully wasted.

Shortsighted thinking can lead to a disappointing future. Lisa and I (Richard) regularly discussed with our children people's flawed thinking and unwise decisions, whether it was in the news or in the town where we lived. Sometimes that meant pointing out mistakes made by their peers. Our intention was not to gossip or to condemn, but to help our children see clearly the graphic consequences of bad decisions.

Teach Your Kids to Think

When I (Carrie) was a teenager, our family doctor told me about her beloved grandfather and how much she had learned from him when she was my age. Every time she and her siblings prepared to go home after visiting him, he would take each one by the shoulders, look directly into their eyes, and say, "THINK." Then he'd kiss them on the forehead and let them go.

Here are some ways to teach your children how to think:

1. Help your children process the actions of those around them.
When Mike and Daniel were teenagers, they had a number of great friends, both male and female. They often hosted "guy nights" at our house where several of the boys would cook disgusting food, play video games or street hockey, shoot baskets, and build a fire in the backyard fire pit.

During their teen years, many of their friends started dating. Most of them still found time to hang out with the guys, but a few would go AWOL once they had a girlfriend. Eventually they would break up with their gal and come back to spend time with the guys again—until they found their next girlfriend. The cycle continued.

I (Richard) once asked my boys what they thought about this on-again off-again buddy system. They said they felt used—like stand-ins until the next girl came along. They assured me that when they started dating, they would make an effort to maintain healthy friendships with other guys. Sure enough, they did.

It's not appropriate to nit-pick and look for faults in your children's friends. However, it is important to help your kids learn

Mom: It takes tact and diplomacy, but you can hold and express strong opinions without necessarily being offensive or annoying.

by processing the actions of those around them. And it is possible to think critically without being judgmental—it's called discernment.

Fictional scenarios in books, television, or movies can provide plenty of talking points for you and your family about values, morality, and decision-making. In addition, the media frequently highlights real-life examples of the disastrous consequences of immoral choices—an athlete is caught doping, or a politician's unethical behavior is exposed. However, your sons and daughters are most influenced by the people they interact with on a daily basis. Therefore, they can avoid numerous pitfalls if you help them evaluate the behavior (and its correlating outcome) of their peers. People have often commented that Lisa and I were fortunate because our children didn't drink alcohol, do drugs, or engage in other damaging behaviors. We are grateful that they didn't, but it wasn't a fluke of good fortune. The fact is that we expended a great deal of effort helping them learn to recognize—and avoid—destructive behavior.

2. Surround your children with thinkers.

Be intentional about introducing your children to interesting people. Invite well-read or widely traveled acquaintances to your home.

Rather than shooing your children away while the adults visit, invite your kids to listen in. I (Richard) have fond memories from my childhood of fascinating guests who sat at our dinner table. These people held me spellbound as they recounted amazing experiences and described exotic places. I learned that the world was much larger than my little neighborhood.

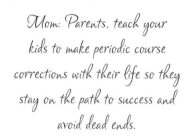

Mom: Parents, teach your kids to make periodic course corrections with their life so they stay on the path to success and avoid dead ends.

Another way to expose your children to deep thinkers is by encouraging them to read great books. We had a standing offer in our home: "If you will read it, we will buy it." That led to a house décor that was distinctly neo-classical Bodleian Library. We had books spilling off shelves in every room of the house. Proverbs 13:20 promises, "He who walks with wise men will be wise." By promoting good literature, our family walked with the giants of history. Often those books sparked discussions and debates around our kitchen table.

It's easy to fall short when it comes to teaching our children to think, especially if we rely on the education system to do it for us. At home, it's less stressful for most parents to turn on the TV than it is to persuade their children to read. Fun family times are important, but being the reigning champion of Mario Kart or Mafia Wars is not

Mom: "No problem can withstand the assault of sustained thinking."
— Voltaire

necessarily going to help you navigate the complex pathways of life. Spending time as a family watching Monday Night Football might provide some bonding moments, but it probably won't expand the capacity of your children's cerebral cortex.

3. Encourage your kids to argue with you.

George Patton once said, "If everybody is thinking alike, then somebody isn't thinking."

I (Carrie) am an opinionated person. Though I don't always voice my views, I try to take an informed stance on controversial issues that crop up in society. My dad has always pressed my brothers and me to form our own opinions and then to be prepared to back them up with facts and careful thought. He takes great pleasure in seeing how strong our convictions are and how well we can defend them. Regardless of the topic (and his own view), he always plays devil's advocate.

Mom: Don't be afraid to let your kids argue with you. You might learn something.

After a teenage Christian friend of mine got into an accident with his parents' car because he had been drinking and driving, I made a pretty strong statement to my dad:

Carrie: I don't know how you can be a Christian and drink alcohol.

Dad: Well that's an interesting viewpoint. As far as I know, Jesus was a Christian, and he apparently made wine for a party, didn't he?

Carrie: Dad! That's different. In Jesus' day, the wine wasn't nearly as strong in alcohol content as it is today. And Jesus certainly never got drunk! Or drove on multi-lane freeways after drinking.

Dad: Carrie, what about all of the Christians around the world, such as in Europe, who do drink? Are you saying they aren't really Christians?

Carrie: Well, obviously I can't speak for everyone in the world who claims to be a Christian. But didn't the apostle Paul say he would not eat meat if it caused someone to stumble? Alcohol has caused incredible amounts of suffering and violence and damage in America. I don't see how any Christian in America could see how much suffering alcohol causes and then not do as Paul did, and abstain from it.

Dad: I commend you for your conviction. But don't you think you are being too harsh on others who don't necessarily share your convictions?

Carrie: No. I think anyone who takes the Bible seriously and who sees what alcohol does to people, won't drink.

Dad: What if you discovered that your boyfriend drank occasionally?

Carrie: He wouldn't be my boyfriend anymore.

Over the years, we had conversations like that one. Our discussions covered numerous topics. Sometimes we bantered about ethics, theology, or worldviews; at other times, we focused on matters pertaining to church, school, or politics. Dad always pushed me to defend my opinion. By the end of every debate, I realized there were facets of the topic that I had never considered before. I also had a firmer grasp of the issues, and my own opinion.

The point here isn't about whether my opinion was right or wrong. (The only debate I clearly won with him was when he tried to argue for the legitimacy of using puns as an acceptable form of humor.) I always knew that Dad wasn't trying to be argumentative. He just wanted me to know how to think through deep issues. And thanks to our debates, I developed the skill of supporting my convictions.

4. Be a role model for lifelong learning.

Wisdom has little to do with IQ and a lot to do with a desire to learn. Lisa and I (Richard) felt it was crucial to model a love for learning in our home. There are numerous opportunities for parents to immerse their children in discovery—like watching informative documentaries with them, going outside to explore God's creation, and taking trips to the zoo, museums, science centers, and historical sites.

Be a co-learner with your kids. Don't just send them off to lessons—acquire new skills along with them. To get you thinking, here are some of the lessons Lisa and I took with our children: skiing, surfing, tennis, cooking, skating, ceramics, painting, astronomy, and crafts. The possibilities are endless. When your child sees you enjoying the process of learning new skills or acquiring knowledge, you are setting a powerful, positive example for them.

Mom: There is an enormous difference between not knowing something and being stupid.

Conclusion

Lisa and I (Richard) purposefully pointed out dangerous ideas and harmful behaviors, as well as the corresponding negative consequences to our children. If we sit back and assume teachers, coaches, and youth leaders will teach our children to make wise decisions, we are short- changing our kids. Of course, all of those people can help, as can grandparents, aunts, and uncles. But that responsibility ultimately belongs to parents.

Living a healthy, God-honoring life requires a great deal of discernment. The consequences of foolishness can be devastating. However, parents have multitudinous opportunities to help their children avoid disastrous decision making, if they will teach them what foolishness looks like and how to avoid it. That's not easy, but it can ultimately save your child enormous heartache.

Mom: There's a significant difference between letting your kids think for themselves and teaching them to think for themselves.

Reflect and Respond

1. What is one thing you are currently doing to encourage your children to think for themselves? Are there other opportunities you may be overlooking? Write them down. Plan to make the necessary adjustments so your children are regularly encouraged to expand their thinking ability.

2. How are you helping your children recognize unwise assumptions and the resulting harmful behaviors? Look for an example this week (perhaps in the news or on TV) that demonstrates faulty reasoning, deceitful practices, or cutting corners in a way that can cause harm to others.

3. Consider the last couple of family conversations you have had around the kitchen table. What have they been about? What does that tell you? How might you raise the quality of your family time to a higher level?

4. How prominent are books in your house? What is the last good book you read personally? What are your children reading? If you are not a reader, what is another way you might enjoy learning something new?

5. What might you do to stimulate your own thinking? How might that inspire your children?

Action Ideas

1. Brainstorm as a family about dangerous or foolhardy behavior you have observed around you lately. (Emphasize that you are not trying to put others down, but to identify unwise behavior.) Ask your children why they think certain actions are unwise. Make note of what your kids identify, and what they do not think is foolish behavior.

2. If you watch sitcoms on television, list the behaviors that are portrayed by TV families that you consider to be foolish and that go against Biblical principles. Perhaps evaluate which programs, in light of your study, you want your children exposed to.

3. On the next family drive, use the time to, as parents, reminisce about some of the most foolish things you did

as children. Children typically love to hear stories like this about their parents. Be sure not to glamorize the behavior, but explain how you realized that behavior was foolish and maybe even dangerous. Invite your kids to share their stories if they'd like.

4. If your children are old enough, have them do Internet research to find the most foolish thing someone has done. They may uncover stories about inept thieves or inventions gone wrong or other blunders. Have each person share what they found and then talk about why people do foolish things.

5. Call a family meeting. As a group, identify something your whole family can learn together. Perhaps it involves going on a family field trip or taking a class together. Make a plan for your family to do that activity.

Chapter Four

If You Hate It, Quit

Rebelling Against Pointless Perseverance

"

Success is not final, failure is not fatal: it is the courage to continue that counts. "

—*Winston Churchill*

Dropout: a Ballet in Two Parts

I (Carrie) was six years old. I gripped the back of a chair and braced myself for the imminent pain. *Think about something else.*

Tears welled up in my eyes as my mom yanked and pulled at my hair. Resistance was futile. Monday evenings meant ballet lessons, and ballerinas must have perfect buns.

Mom's fingers tugged at my tangled curls and the bobby pins dug into my scalp. Then she sprayed hairspray so liberally I could have danced through an EF5 tornado with my hair intact. I squirmed and tugged at my bodysuit—it always bunched up in the back. Mom reminded me that little ladies never fiddle with their bodysuits in public. The tights itched as if an army of spiders was crawling up and down my legs.

"Okay, time to go!" My mom set down the hairbrush, picked up her jangling keys, and rushed me out to the car, dainty pink slippers in hand.

On the drive, my stomach churned. I didn't want to go to that stuffy old studio again. I hated ballet. Mike and Daniel got to stay home and watch *Ninja Turtles*, while I was stuck in a room full of girls doing the same boring exercises again and again. A new teacher had replaced Madame Michelle, and this one wasn't as nice.

The cruelest irony of all was that I'd begged to sign up for the class because the sparkly tutus bedazzled me. No one bothered to inform me that only the big girls got to wear those. Same with pointe shoes.

We turned onto the familiar street, and tears dribbled down my cheeks.

"Mom, can I please skip this week?"

I asked every week and always got the same answer. "Just give it more time, sweetie. You'll grow to love it. Besides, they award a prize at the end of the year for perfect attendance." It was a one-two punch. She knew I loved prizes—any prize at all. But it was November, and the year-end recital was in May. To a six-year-old, that was at least two lifetimes.

I sighed and dried my tears. But apparently, my mom was tired of the weekly ordeal, too. She drove past the studio entrance and kept going. We ended up at the ice cream parlor. Over a double scoop of cookie dough ice cream, she confessed that waiting for me in the lobby was a miserable experience because several of the other moms lived and breathed *dance*. They would talk about nothing but their princess, who was sure to be the next Karen Kain. We never went back. That is my first memory of the exhilarating experience of quitting.

A couple of years later, I went to my first figure skating lesson. Figure skaters got to wear even sparklier dresses than ballerinas! With a firm grasp on the sideboard, I took my first hesitant step onto the glassy surface, and then another. I let go and ventured out into my new life. The cool air tickled my cheeks, and I felt like an angel floating above the ground. I looked beautiful in the glittery yellow skating dress my mom bought me to wear for practice. I lost my balance on the fourth stride, and I felt the hard ice with my backside.

Laughing, I brushed the snow off my dress and pushed myself back to my feet to try again.

A figure skating fanatic was born. For the next eight years, I practiced four times a week. Quitting never crossed my mind. In high school, I joined a synchronized skating team with 15 other girls. We practiced early morning all winter. The arena was in a nearby town, so that meant a 30-minute drive in the

Mom: Forcing our children to persevere in an activity they hate is training them to settle for mediocrity and misery.

dark. Sometimes we had to set out by 6:00 a.m. because the roads were icy. But even though I was often tired, cold, and sore, I never missed practice. At times the rehearsals were tedious, and some of the girls on my team could be catty, but I committed myself to the team and was determined to work hard.

It was amazing! We traveled to numerous competitions. We wore dazzling costumes. We even won several medals. If there had been a prize for perfect attendance, I would have won it.

One of the defining moments in my life was the day my mom gave me permission to quit.

So What's the Problem?

Some parenting decisions are no-brainers: Should parents let their kids stay up late watching a Planet of the Apes movie marathon on a school night? Should they feed their children a mound of gummy bears for dinner? The black and white issues rarely trip us up, but other parenting issues are less clear-cut. Conventional wisdom fails us when we treat a grey area as black or white.

Mom: Let's not train our children to equate quitting with giving up. The former is a choice; the latter is a response.

Here's an example: Everywhere we go today, there are motivational slogans. We find them posted in classrooms, at fitness centers, on the Internet, and on t-shirts:

"I can do it if I stick to it."

"She believed she could, so she did."

"If you believe in yourself, anything is possible."

"Believe you can, and you will."

"Nothing can stop you from achieving your goal."

"Winners never quit and quitters never win."

"It's always too soon to quit."

Every one of these maxims is true in a certain context. On the other hand, every one of them is false in other settings. Trust me, I (Richard) will never be able to sing on key, no matter how hard I try or how much I believe in myself.

The problem is not in the sayings, but in the way we apply them.

It is deeply ingrained into our psyches that quitting is for the jellyfish of society and should be avoided like Chinese bird flu. Where would America be if George Washington had given up at Valley Forge? What would life be like if Thomas Edison quit inventing just before he figured out electric light?

The famous rousing speech delivered by Winston Churchill as he mobilized the Allies during WWII is often quoted to inspire the fainthearted: "Never give in. Never give in. Never, never, never, never—in nothing, great or small, large or petty—never give in, except to convictions of honor and good sense. Never yield to force. Never yield to the apparently overwhelming might of the enemy."

Motivational speakers love to include the first part of his speech in their rally cry as they urge their listeners not to quit. Most of them omit Churchill's caveats: having honorable convictions and good sense.[3]

In some circumstances, refusing to give in is a sign of strength because it involves refusing to capitulate to an enemy. But in other cases, refusing to give in is merely a sign of stubbornness.

Is persistence always noble? What about children who struggle through years of monotonous piano lessons, when their passion is for the drums? Or students who were advised to major in math, only to find studying for multivariable calculus as futile as trying to order a low carb, balanced meal at KFC? What about teenaged girls who keep trying to make their relationship with a boyfriend work, even when all the evidence suggests he is a dishonest, lazy, blowhard?

---

3 Churchill was a brilliant leader, but he also said, "...I leave when the pub closes."

Refusing to quit is noble if you are trying to complete your education. On the other hand, it may be mere vanity if you continually experience failure but refuse to alter your course.

It's in the Bible

Perseverance is a Biblical virtue, but the benefits of quitting show up quite often in the Bible as well. Noah ceased building boats after a storied career and became a farmer (Genesis 9:20). Elisha left farming to become a prophet (1 Kings 19:19-21). Abram walked away from his life in Haran and entered the Promised Land (Genesis12:1-3). David stopped shepherding and ultimately became a king (1 Samuel 16:18-23).

Then there are the famous sibling sets from the New Testament: Peter and Andrew, and James and John. They fished. That was their training, livelihood, and foreseeable future. One day, Jesus showed up and told them to quit fishing. Can you picture Peter replying, "No offense Rabbi, but we have always been taught that quitting is bad, and perseverance is godly. It was even a slogan in my third grade classroom. So we can't leave our fishing boats. Our parents are counting us to take over the business. It would be wrong to quit."

Imagine how many times people miss divine opportunities because they are too scared to leave what they are doing in order to go with God.

What's a Parent to Do?

When it comes to guiding their children, parents need to ensure they have their priorities straight. Many goals are worth protracted effort, like learning to read, getting in good physical condition, or finishing college. Other activities aren't worth the pain involved in doing them over and over again. Walking repeatedly into a brick wall may demonstrate perseverance, but it's not very smart. Maybe the effort you or your child is channeling in one direction would be better spent if you quit and started something new.

Children need help navigating life's complex decisions. They have numerous opportunities and yet must discern which ones are right for them. Piano lessons, baseball, ballet, figure skating, football, hiking, kayaking, and horseback riding can all provide tremendous experiences for children. But which, if any, are suited for your children? You would hate to force your child to do something that was good if it cost them the opportunity to do what was best. Here are some guidelines that might assist you as you help your child determine if it is time to quit:

1. Identify the greater good.

We must reiterate that we do not think it is good for children to quit every time they have a "bad" day or don't feel like practicing. Perseverance is a great quality. However, it is not the only character trait parents must cultivate in their children.

For example, we mentioned at the beginning of this chapter that Carrie quit ballet. Some parents would be mortified that Lisa and I (Richard) allowed our child to "bail" midway through a season. They might argue that Carrie should have learned to "stick it out" when the going got tough. And, in some cases, this would indeed be the highest good. But Carrie was enrolled in ballet so she could learn to work in a team, to get some exercise, and to have a chance to excel at something that developed her confidence. The objective was not ballet, but to find an activity that accomplished these goals. A broader goal we had for Carrie was to teach her to make wise choices with her life.

> *Mom: Parents communicate their priorities to their children, whether they mean to or not.*

If we had adamantly insisted that Carrie keep taking lessons she loathed, we would have a) invited a showdown with our daughter every week, b) demoralized her by forcing her to do something she hated, and c) humiliated her by having her lag behind those with a passion for dancing. True, we could have forced our daughter to persevere, but we would have failed to help achieve her most important goals.

When we let Carrie quit ballet, we accomplished several things. *First*, she learned that she is ultimately in control of her life. If she is miserable with her current circumstances, she can change them. *Second*, we freed her time so she could discover a sport in which she could thrive. Becoming a skilled ice skater did far more for Carrie's confidence than persevering as a mediocre ballerina would have accomplished. Our childhood is too brief to fill it with activities that stifle our spirit and rob our joy. *Third*, if we had made Carrie persevere with ballet, we would have to wage war with her every week. Instead, we ended up with a child who loved her sport, loved to practice, and loved her parents. Sounded like a win/win to us! Was learning perseverance important for Carrie? Certainly. And once she found a sport worth persevering in, Carrie developed that character trait, too.

2. Know when enough is enough.

"No pain; no gain," so the oft-used saying goes. To a certain extent, that is true. You can't excel at football, golf, or piano if you never practice. You can't earn a diploma if you don't grind it out taking exams and writing papers. You don't develop depth of character by coasting through an easy life. A certain degree of discomfort is required if you want to enjoy life to the fullest. Not all tears are bad, nor should every difficult experience be avoided. But there's a limit.

The first time your daughter complains that she is sick of practicing the piano, you don't need to race to her teacher's studio and exclaim that you will no longer need his services. The first time your son declares he'd rather stay home and watch cartoons than go to soccer practice, you don't need to immediately call the coach and alert him to the vacancy on his roster. Kids often need a little encouragement to do what they should.

I (Richard) remember being informed as an eleven-year-old that my beloved mother had registered me to play basketball in the city's recreational league. I had never played basketball before, and she had just signed me up for a team that had been together for two years. I was livid. I was indignant. I was scared! I'd look like a fool on the court. I argued and pleaded with my mother to cancel my enrollment. She didn't. Instead, she grabbed a broom and batted me out the door to practice! To my surprise, I discovered I enjoyed playing basketball. Eventually I became pretty good at it. I ended up playing in two different leagues for years afterward. In that case, allowing me to quit after my first-time jitters would have been a huge mistake.

On the other hand, my mother also had me take piano lessons when I was a child. Mom loved playing the piano and she wanted me to love it, too, so she found the most respected piano teacher in the city. This lady had been teaching piano for eons (rumor had it that Mozart was one of her first students). Mrs. Horroritz proudly declared that she could teach *anyone* to play the piano. I tried to practice. Through grit, determination, and sheer force of will, I eventually clawed my way into Learner's Book 2. But that was all I had in me. One day my saintly teacher met my mother at the door and suggested that she consider withdrawing me from piano and enrolling me in baseball, and at her earliest convenience. I had tried. I had given it my best shot. But piano simply wasn't for me. I never regretted that decision (and neither did Mrs. Horroritz).

It's difficult to know whether to encourage your children to forge ahead or to quit when:

- Your daughter cries every day before school

- Your son has to be dragged to baseball practice every week

- Your daughter merely goes through the motions of practicing the clarinet and is making minimal progress

- Your son complains each week that he has no friends on his team and he wants to quit

At what point do you recognize as a parent that there is too much pain associated with your child's activity and precious little gain? How many arguments, shouting matches, and tears must be endured before you realize it is time to cut your losses and find an activity that energizes your child's soul? Parents not only encourage their children to keep their eyes on their most important goals, but they also help them recognize when something isn't working.

3. Take control of your life.

On July 29, 1981, an estimated 750 million people around the world were anchored to their television screens to watch a highly anticipated public event: the royal wedding of Prince Charles to Lady Diana Spencer. The beautiful young bride, soon-to-be Princess Diana, was living the dream that millions of little girls long for. Only her closest confidants knew about her pre-wedding doubts. Barely 20 years old, she suspected that her prince was in love with someone else. She confided her fears to her sister, who reportedly told her she had no choice but to go through with the wedding. "Too late," she said, "your face is already on the tea towels." (Spoiler alert, in case you're an alien from a different galaxy: Diana was right.)

In fairy tales, the princess lives happily after, but real life is not as simple. If Diana had heeded her doubts and ended her doomed romance, she may have saved herself a lot of pain and heartbreak. Sadly, she was told that quitting was not an option. So she continued on an unhealthy path that would ultimately cost her years of unhappiness.

The act of quitting places the responsibility for your happiness in your own hands as a result of your own choices. Parents need to encourage their children to know themselves and to make decisions that enable them to thrive.

4. Be honest about what is behind your decision.

Children as well as parents need to be honest about their reasons for persevering or quitting. Sometimes children want to quit for less than stellar reasons. But it is also important for parents to be honest about why they want their child to persevere. Sometimes those reasons aren't so noble, either.

I (Richard) remember when Carrie told me she wanted to quit attending a private school and begin homeschooling. It was early November. Despite the fact that she presented a compelling list of reasons why homeschooling was best for her, I was initially resistant. I had my reasons:

1. I had already paid a year's tuition for Carrie. It was non-refundable. It seemed good stewardship to finish out the year, since it was already paid for. That way, I wouldn't waste my hard-earned money.

2. I was serving on the board of trustees for that school. How could I explain to the board that I was stepping down because my daughter was quitting school?

3. I was the president of a graduate school. I believed in schools. I thought it would look awkward for me to be encouraging enrollment at my school while my own child did not attend an educational institution herself.

4. I didn't like the idea of Lisa being indefinitely tied down at home trying to educate our daughter when there was a perfectly good private school available.

5. I suspected that homeschooling would require me to be more involved in my child's education, and I didn't have time.

For these reasons, I asked Carrie to carefully reconsider her desire to homeschool. However, I had always taught Carrie to think, and so she had. She pushed back on *my* reasoning. The truth was, all of my concerns for Carrie's schooling centered on *me*. I was worried about wasting *my* money. I was concerned about what people would think of *me*. I was trying to protect *my* time. When I pulled myself out of the equation and simply thought about what was best for my daughter, it was clear we should give it a shot.

If they were honest, many parents would confess that their *primary* reasons for not allowing their child to quit something is because of finances or personal reluctance to get involved, or both. Perhaps they have paid their child's registration fees, and now they are determined to get their money's worth. Or, they fear that changing schools, or hobbies, or programs, or teams will involve too much effort on their part. Let's be frank: Parents can be driven to their parenting method of choice because of what is easiest for them, rather than what is best for their child. Finances and time constraints are legitimate considerations in family decision-making, and I'm not minimizing that reality. But if parents are willing to be creative and make adjustments to help their children, most problems can be worked out. In fact, and to my surprise, pulling Carrie out of the school system saved me a lot of time and money in the long run, and our decision opened up multiple opportunities for me to spend time traveling with her and pursuing interests we shared. Her decision was best for me, too. I just didn't know it at the time.

Challenge

Has your parenting been hampered by your perspective on quitting? Have you viewed perseverance as the ultimate good and robbed your children of the opportunity to make necessary modifications in their lives? Knowing when to quit—and having the courage to follow through—is a struggle at any age. Here are some examples to inspire you:

A visually impaired child started piano lessons at age six, and music became his passion. But conventional wisdom said, "No one makes a living as a musician." So, when he grew up, he entered law school. He trudged through his education and eventually graduated. Then, he established a law practice. He hated it. After a year, he summoned the courage to give up law and pursue a music career full-time, despite the hurdles he knew he would face. Though it took years of persistence in the music industry to catch a break, Andrea Bocelli never returned to his law practice.

A young mother from New Jersey began working as a stockbroker on Wall Street. But, after helping her husband restore an old farmhouse and cooking through Julia Child's *Mastering the Art of French Cooking*, she made a major career change, abandoning the stockbroking world to pursue culinary arts and interior design. It took a while to pick up steam in her new profession, but Martha Stewart had found her calling.

If either of these people had refused to quit, they may have gotten by, but they would have missed out on a more satisfying life.

Conclusion

One of the most contentious issues for parents is whether to allow or even encourage their child to pull out of an activity. Many parents have a deep-seated aversion to the word "quit." Their own parents may have taught them to stick with a commitment or a routine, regardless of how disagreeable or unfulfilling it was.

Hopefully, you've received our message correctly. We're not implying that at the first sign of adversity, you should yank your child out of a school, a sport, or any other pursuit. But sometimes, just knowing there are options helps you decide whether the current direction you are taking is the right one for you and your family.

The main thing is to be proactive about your family's decisions, and not just mindlessly succumb to what everyone else is doing.

Reflect and Respond

1. Are you aware of a desire your children might have that they have not specifically vocalized? If it is a worthy and attainable goal, write down some ways you can help them achieve it.

2. Have you taught your children that it is sometimes wise to quit? If so, how have they learned this from you?

3. Recall a time when you helped one of your children avoid a damaging or dangerous relationship. What are some ways you are teaching your children to respect themselves?

4. Do you prize perseverance more highly than other qualities, such as self-respect or healthy discrimination? How might that affect your children?

5. Does one of your children want to quit something? Do you feel the issue might be similar to what has been discussed in this chapter? If so, what do you plan to do next?

Action Ideas

1. If you and/or your children have a tendency to overload yourself physically or emotionally, perhaps consider reading the helpful book, Boundaries: When to Say Yes, How to Say No to Take Control of your Life, by Henry Cloud and John Townsend.

2. Make a list of all the activities in which your children are currently enrolled. On a scale of 1 to 5, with 1 being "very beneficial" and 5 being "not beneficial at all," rate each activity. Carefully consider what to do about activities that are not having the desired effect. Be sure to consider your child's perspective and not just your own.

3. At the end of each school year, make an appointment with each child individually. Discuss the extra-curricular activities they participated in the previous year. Talk through the issues related to signing back up for another year. Does your child feel ready to try something new? Help your children make choices so they schedule the most important activities on their calendar before the new school year.

Chapter Five

Not Now, Sweetie: Mommy Is Having a Meltdown
Rebelling Against Self-Centered Living

"I thank God that I am as honest as any man living that is an old man and no honester than I."
—William Shakespeare

The Pain of It All!

I (Carrie) didn't inherit my dad's aptitude for sports...at all. He played soccer, hockey, softball, volleyball, racquetball, and basketball, and was even the captain of one of his high school teams. That was many years ago, but he's still a pretty good athlete for an old guy. Connecting a fork to my mouth stretches my hand-eye coordination to the far reaches of my ability. The only time I ever beat my dad in a sport was a round of Ping Pong the day I failed my road test for the second time. He and my mom had a "special talk" in the kitchen before the game. Coincidentally, my dad briefly developed a habit of serving the ball into the net.

One summer, Dad and I decided to try something new: rollerblading.

We found a graffiti-smeared rollerblade/skateboard shop. The proprietor, a shaggy-haired teenaged boy, fitted us with the proper boots and wheels. He offered to demonstrate a couple of techniques, but we were antsy to get out on the open road. That afternoon, we went for the inaugural spin around our neighborhood.

Usually, before I try a new sport, my dad gives me a pep-talk/ counseling session about how he *knows* I'm going to do well, but that I should keep in mind that God gifted us all differently. While one person might be great at [*fill in the blank with whichever sport we are attempting*], others might be talented at origami folding, stamp collecting, or coupon clipping. On good days, he weaves Paul's lesson on "body parts" of the church into his lecture in a way only a fifth-generation Baptist preacher can.

This particular time, he kept it brief. "We don't have to go too fast, and if you get tired or want to stop, just let me know. I'll be right here." He patted my shoulder gently.

I tightened my laces and sped down the street. My feet wobbled at first, but my ice skating experience helped me keep balanced. I slipped into a nice rhythm, taking long strides. This was easier than I thought it would be.

At the end of the street, a dip in the road loomed. It had looked deceptively small from the car window, but it appeared much steeper now as I approached. My blood pulsed. I began to pick up speed quickly, but then I leaned back into the brake on my left skate and started regaining my balance, slowing to a manageable speed.

I'd lost track of my dad. Then, I noticed a bulky blur in my peripheral vision. I turned just in time to see my dad's six-foot-two, 200-plus pound body rocketing through the air like an over-the-hill Superman. He reached an altitude that usually requires communication with air traffic control. His legs thrashed in the air as he fought against Newtonian gravitational pull, and he crash-landed and skidded along the blacktop.

I stood frozen in shock for a moment. Then I hurriedly skated over to where Dad lay in a dazed, bloodied heap.

"Dad, are you okay?"

No answer.

"Dad?"

No answer.

"Dad, why didn't you use your brakes?"

He moaned. "What brakes?"

I wish I could say my inner Florence Nightingale kicked in and that I nursed him tenderly as any good daughter would. I should have summoned immediate medical attention, or at least tried to staunch the bleeding. I should have been weighed down by survivor's guilt. But the image of my brave, strong Dad soaring overhead like a distressed jumbo jet set off convulsions of crippling laughter.

We eventually made it back to the house where, between outbursts of crazed mirth, I patched his broken, hemorrhaging body.

I discovered an important lesson that day. Dads bleed. Who knew?

So What's the Problem?

Sooner or later, every child has to grapple with the reality that Mom and Dad aren't perfect. To preserve domestic harmony, many parents would rather it be later. It seems logical to protect young ones as long as possible from life's unpleasant realities, such as ill health, a lost job, or

Mom: Parents, your kids already know you aren't perfect, so you might as well admit it, and have a good laugh!

a skeleton in the family closet, so these parents shield their children from as much unpleasantness as possible.

Other parents prefer transparency. When there is a clash of opinions, Mom and Dad have it out freely (and loudly) in front of the kids. Their marriage is an open book; they readily retell what's going on in their workplace; they don't hide the ups and downs of their friendships; a relative's problem is everyone's business.

Which approach is best?

In our observation, Christian parents tend to encourage their children to confide in them about their concerns, but these same parents often keep their own difficulties private, to avoid burdening their children. My (Richard) dad, Henry, used to say, "I take my faith to my family and my problems to God."

What was your experience growing up? Perhaps there were periods of uneasy silence in your home when you felt tension in the air but couldn't pin down the source. Or veiled references concerning "Uncle _____'s embarrassing problem." What about when Mom and Dad weren't getting along? You may have noticed "closed door meetings" in your home—the kind where raised voices are overheard emanating from the next room, but eventually your parents emerge and act as if nothing happened.

How much should parents share with their children about their troubled pasts, current personal problems, or financial circumstances? We've asked numerous people for their views about the level of transparency in their home. Their feedback pointed to three main reasons why parents are reluctant to be completely honest with their kids:

- It might make them insecure (financial problems or a parent's depression).

- They could lose respect for their parents (Dad got fired once...or twice).

- Parents don't want their children to use past mistakes as permission to experiment with the same vice (Mom or Dad tried it, so why can't I?).

This complicated issue hinges greatly on the age and maturity of the children. But, let's face it, kids see, hear, and notice things. And the conclusions they draw on their own can often be more harmful or frightening than if they knew the truth. It takes wisdom to find a healthy balance between enlightening our family and overloading them.

It's in the Bible

A Roman centurion named Cornelius served in the Italian Cohort, stationed in the city of Caesarea. Centurions were the backbone of the Roman legions. They were tough leaders of men, intimately familiar with deadly conflict. Cornelius was troubled and seeking peace with God, so he sent for the apostle Peter, who was in the nearby town of Joppa. Cornelius was so eager for answers to his pressing questions that he gathered his relatives and friends so they could share his experience. When Peter entered the house, Cornelius, the hardened soldier, fell at the apostle's feet out of respect (Acts 10:25-26).

Cornelius could have met with Peter discreetly at a local bagel shop. He might have limited his initial meeting with the apostle to just himself and his wife. But there he was, a veteran soldier whose livelihood and reputation depended upon others' respect, making himself vulnerable in front of his family and friends. What would his lieutenants think? What impression would this leave on his children? What about his father-in-law? His wife? This powerful man humbled himself in the presence of his family and friends, because he longed to see God work in his life.

Wouldn't it have been great having Cornelius for a dad? He was obviously physically tough and he held a powerful position—he could issue life or death orders to soldiers. But Cornelius chose to be candid about his own needs and shortcomings, so when God changed his life, his family, friends, associates, and subordinates all felt the impact (Acts 10:44-48).

Chilling Out on Christmas

We all struggle for victory in different areas of our life. Growing up, I (Richard) burned off calories as fast as I could ingest them. If anything, I was usually too skinny, so I never learned to watch my weight, and I gave little thought to healthy eating. Quite simply, if it was within arm's reach and edible, I consumed it. That was a long time ago. Now, my travel schedule involves eating out a lot and sitting around in meetings or on airplanes. Over the years, the pounds began to sneak up on me, but I barely adjusted my eating habits. I would make solemn pronouncements to my family about cutting back, especially on dessert. That was well and good, until a gracious Southern hostess at the church where I was speaking carted out homemade pie and ice cream. Pie is to me what kryptonite is to Superman; when I'm near it, I lose my superpowers. The younger generation is better informed about nutrition than most of their parents, and my children have gently but consistently encouraged me to back away from the dessert table and to enjoy a nice juicy carrot stick instead. My daughter can contort her pretty eyes into amazing shapes when she sees my plate as I beat a hasty retreat from a buffet table. I genuinely welcome the input from my kids as they help me break some longstanding unhealthy habits.

Another predisposition that trips me up is my task-oriented nature. It drives me crazy to leave unanswered emails fermenting in my inbox. One Christmas morning, our family had enjoyed a delightful time opening presents, followed by a hearty breakfast (cooked by yours truly, as was our tradition). Then everyone scattered to take showers and try on their new clothes. I slipped into my study to check my emails, but was interrupted by an accusing voice: "Are you WORKING on Jesus' birthday?"

It was Carrie. She pulled me out of the room and hastily constructed a crime-scene style barrier using masking tape and a felt marker. There it remained for the rest of the day, spanning the doorway to stymie any attempts at re-entry: NO ADMITTANCE— THIS MEANS YOU, DAD.

In some families, children know better than to point out any shortcoming to their parents. Constructive feedback only flows one way. I'm glad I was open with my kids about my struggles, because while it confirmed their suspicions that I was less than perfect, it also allowed them to express their love and concern for me. After all, who better than my kids to help make their father a better man?

Challenge

We've mentioned three reasons parents can be reluctant to disclose certain information to their children. Our instinct is to protect our kids and preserve their innocence. We don't want them to lose respect for us. We may be fearful that they'll use our previous misdeeds to justify committing the same sins. Whether the issue relates to our personal weaknesses or our less-than-stellar past, or if we're dealing with a problem caused by circumstances beyond our control, we must certainly be mindful of our motive for sharing. We also need to take into account the maturity level of the child.

However, there are also potential benefits for children if parents choose to be upfront with them about our problems.

1. They will see the correct perspective.

Most little kids see their dad as the biggest, smartest, strongest man on the planet (at least he was at our house!). After all, he's the undisputed alpha male in the family. He knows everything. And Mom can solve any problem; in fact, she lives to solve her children's problems and meet their needs. Of course, the reason she can focus on everyone else is because she doesn't have any needs of her own. However, in a normal household, it gradually becomes apparent that adults have difficulties too, but parents often try to perpetuate the façade of invincibility for as long as possible. But here's the thing: children have a tendency to compare themselves unfavorably to their "perfect" parents, or at least they did in our home. Here's an example:

A Dark and Stormy Day

Every child knows there is only one day of the year worse than the annual dentist checkup. A day when an eerie darkness covers the face of the earth and there is a bone-tingling chill in the air. Birds don't sing. Dogs howl. Faith is tested. Heaven (specifically the Rapture) is prominent in people's thoughts. It is the day the teacher sends home report cards.

I (Carrie) remember one such bleak occasion. I was in elementary school and my brothers were in middle school. We were reasonably smart kids, but sometimes we had trouble applying ourselves to our homework. It wasn't that we didn't want to do well. But so many things vied for our attention besides grammar and arithmetic—such as the fly buzzing around our heads, epic staring contests, and spinning each other in the office chair to see who got sick first. Consequently, homework and studying were occasionally neglected.

I was a better student than my brothers, but I dreaded report cards as much as the next kid. For one thing, I'm left-handed and I had a tendency to reverse my letters. Then there was the curse of cursive writing. I think schools have finally given up on teaching that, but when we went through school, it was still a big deal. Mike's handwriting was sloppy, Daniel's was so small it was indiscernible, and being a southpaw, mine always slanted the wrong way. So, we were usually each guaranteed at least one NI (Needs to Improve).

We rode home from school in silence on Report Card Day, our backpacks burdened by the heaviest piece of paper in existence. That evening, the time of reckoning arrived: the ceremonial presenting of the report cards to Dad. As usual, I went first, since mine was the least disappointing.

My grades were good. In several subjects, I earned the coveted HS (Highly Satisfactory) check mark. My behavior was commendable, but there were the usual unflattering comments about letter and number reversal.

Then came Daniel. His grades were okay, but not stellar. Definitely not his best. The behavior section had one NI—"Daniel needs to speak up more in class." He's an introvert, so that wasn't totally unexpected.

Mike went last. Like Daniel, he wasn't failing any subjects, but neither was he performing up to potential. He tried to snatch the page away before Dad could read the comments from various teachers: "Mike tends to enjoy socializing in class when he should be paying attention." "Mike is a chatty student." (He's an extrovert.) "Mike is easily distracted."

When your dad has a Ph.D. and values education like ours does, you can feel like pond scum when you underperform academically. At that time, Dad was the president of a graduate school. We expected him to be horrified by our educational shortcomings. We hung our heads in shame.

Without a word, Dad went into his office and rustled around in his file cabinet. He returned and handed each of us a yellowed, ancient-looking document. He had retrieved copies of his report cards from when he was in our respective grades. After reading them, we realized he was no academic wonder: His grades were actually worse than ours! Did his revelation cause us to sit back, take it easy, and aim low? Actually, it had the opposite effect. We wanted to make up for our

Mom: If your children think you are perfect, you need to lighten up.

poor dad's lack of academic success. Salvage the ol' Blackaby name, if you will. As I recall, we were inspired. Our dad had not coasted through college, grad school, and doctoral studies on his good looks and brilliance (as he likes to pretend), but through tenacity and hard work. All was not lost for us! Learning about his journey inspired us to embrace our own.

2. They can be spared unnecessary worry.

Parents often assume that withholding a painful truth spares a child from needless anxiety. However, young imaginations tend to fill in the blanks if they don't know the real story. Dad might reason, "I'm having a horrible time with my boss, but there's no point in talking about that at home. My teenagers don't care or need to know about my trials at work." But the children may actually be thinking, "Dad sure seems moody and withdrawn lately. He never laughs. I wonder if I've done something to upset him…I wonder if he and Mom are doing okay…"

In trying to shelter our children, we may inadvertently cause them grief. Moreover, we miss a good opportunity to teach them how to handle their own problems and stress in a healthy manner.

3. They can witness a Christ-like response to adversity.

When I (Richard) was a teenager, my father was a respected pastor, well known for his gentle shepherd's heart. Still, he had his detractors. Much of what he did in our church was non-conformist in ministry circles.[4] At one point, a pair of critics distributed false information about Dad that was intended to harm his ministry. Eventually, word

---

4 You can read much of that story in his book, Experiencing God: Knowing and Doing the Will of God (Nashville: LifeWay Press, 2007).

Rebellious Parenting

got back to my dad, along with the identity of those who instigated the rumors. At the time, I was a strapping, six-foot-two hockey player who was ready to grab my hockey stick and chop those men down to size. When I asked my father what he intended to do, I was unprepared for his response. "Nothing," he said. Then, as he often did, he cited Scripture. 1 Samuel 2:30 reads, "For those who honor Me, I will honor; and those who despise Me shall be lightly esteemed." Dad told me that when he began following Christ as a young man, he gave God his reputation. Dad would guard his integrity and leave his reputation in God's hands.

He didn't do anything. A few years later, my father was asked to write a study course that became a Christian classic: *Experiencing God*. It made him well-known and elicited invitations from around the world for him to speak. I learned a valuable lesson watching my father model how to deal with opposition and criticism.

Fast-forward 28 years. I was a school president with three teenage children of my own. Someone took issue with me and sent a disparaging note to every pastor in my denomination, listing my numerous deficiencies along with the perceived evil motives behind each one. My sons asked me what I was going to do. It would be easy to refute the falsehoods. I suspected who the "anonymous" culprit was and could have retaliated.

Instead, I said, "Let me tell you a story about your grandpa and something that happened when I was your age…"

Never waste an opportunity to model a godly attitude. Ask God to help you respond to adversity the right way, not just for your own sake, but to set an example for your family. You never know when one of them may need to draw upon it.

4. *They can learn from our mistakes.*

I (Richard) earlier related some areas in my life where my children were trying to help me. It can be humbling to admit that we have issues in our life. My children always looked up to me, and they relied on me to help them solve their problems. They respected me. They even emulated me.

Those are all reasons why I chose (and still choose) to be vulnerable with them. I want them to take the good stuff they learned at home and thrive because of their upbringing, but I don't want them to repeat the mistakes Lisa and I made and thus pay the price for our poor judgment. Children should not grow up thinking they must live up to an image of a perfect father or mother, because there is no such thing. Rather, I hoped my sons and my daughter would be inspired by their imperfect dad, who accepted all the help he could in his ongoing effort to become a better man.

5. *They can learn compassion.*

When we withhold our pain and struggles from our children, we may be inadvertently teaching them to be self-centered. Children need to learn that they are not the only ones with problems. If we are constantly helping our children with their problems, but never sharing ours with them, they may begin to feel, and act, like they are the center of the universe. At an early age, children ought to learn how to show compassion and lend a helping hand

Mom: Our children have a distinct advantage over us. Only they can stand on our shoulders.

to others. As parents, we are in a unique position to teach this valuable lesson.

Besides being honest about your own flaws, what are some healthy ways to teach your child to have empathy for others? The possibilities are endless, but here are a few ideas:

Mom: It takes less than one minute to write an encouraging note to someone. Even a child can manage that.

1. Help them seek out friends with special needs. All three of our children had friends at school or church who were considered disabled. They learned to look beneath the surface of someone's physical or intellectual limitations and see the fun, gentle side that others often overlooked.

2. Take them with you on a hospital or nursing home visit. I (Carrie) went with my mom on numerous trips to see her younger sister, who lived in a special care home for many years. My aunt contracted a serious illness when she was a young woman. Visiting her involved traveling 2,000 miles to the remote northern Canadian town where she lived. My mom and my other aunts took me and my cousins with them, and as a group, we made an effort to encourage the residents of the nursing home. We'd play games with them, paint their nails, assemble puzzles with them, eat meals with them, and do whatever we could to brighten their day. When you're young, a special care home can be

a daunting place, but my mom taught me what to do and say so I could get past my self-consciousness.

3. Encourage your children to cheer for and support the efforts of their siblings and friends. We live in an imperfect world and no one gets everything they want. Teach them to be gracious when they win as well as when they lose. Help them learn how to be genuinely happy for others who experience success.

Bridezillas

Something I (Carrie) noticed while attending a small Christian university in South Carolina was the attitude toward marriage some of my young female classmates had.

For one thing, they believed that if you're unwed at the ripe age of 21, you probably have a physical deformity or unconfessed sin. I wasn't allowed to date in high school, and I honestly didn't care. I always planned on finishing my education before I got married. I didn't realize that many (though not all) of my female classmates entered the university primarily to find a husband. Freshmen orientation was not merely a chance to learn about the Latin club and intramural activities. It was a hunting ground, where young women fought in a *Hunger Games*-style death match for a spouse. Half the student population had paired off by mid-September. The rest sat alone in their darkened dorm rooms, free-falling into inconsolable despair. The school's unofficial motto was "a ring by spring or your money back."

Those unfortunate females who failed to meet Mr. Wonderful were annoyed with girls who had. I remember when a sweet friend of mine became engaged to a godly young man. When she went to church the Sunday after her engagement, most of the other girls shunned her. Not one of them asked to see her engagement ring, wished her well, or acknowledged this major milestone. Instead they moped and slunk around so visibly upset you'd think they were sipping vinegar while passing kidney stones. These unattached young women would listlessly attend church functions, muttering anguished comments such as, "One day, if I ever find a husband…" or, "I guess I just need to have lots of cats since I'm going to be a stoop-backed, snaggle-toothed spinster…"

> *Mom: The sign of a gracious heart is when you are genuinely happy for others when they get what you wanted.*

But here's the worst part. Many of them had mothers who were (publicly and privately) pressuring them to "find a husband and settle down." Rather than helping their daughters graciously celebrate when their friends found happiness, these mothers were driving their daughters into self-absorbed despair. Ironically, by embracing their angst and self-pity, these young women made themselves less attractive to suitors. What guy wants to devote his life to making a self-centered woman happy?

Life is not a Disney movie. Children need to see that everyone has problems. They should be taught to empathize with others as soon as they are old enough to understand how, so they grow up to be thoughtful, gracious adults.

Conclusion

Over the years, Lisa and I (Richard) have both dealt with personal struggles—some of them were health-related, and others were matters of circumstances or willpower. We've had painful relationships, pressures at work, and challenges with our finances. At times, we needed to ask for our children's forgiveness. When we were transparent with our children, they were always remarkably understanding and supportive. In fact, they often offered creative solutions. More than once they expressed relief that we weren't dying, divorcing, or heading to the poorhouse! We tried not to burden them with adult problems, but at the same time, we wanted to show them respect by being honest with them. Rather than costing us our children's esteem, it generally led them to hold us in higher regard.

Your three-year-old probably doesn't need to know about the loss you recently experienced in your retirement portfolio, nor does your teenager want to hear about the suffering you endured after you ate Mexican food. But they should be getting to know you as their parent. They need to understand that you are real, and that you bleed just like everyone else. If they get to journey with you through some of the difficult times in your life, there is a good chance they will grow up to become thoughtful, considerate people who bring comfort to others.

Mom: Treat your children with respect and they will act respectfully.

Reflect and Respond

1. On a scale of 1 to 10, how open are you with your children about problems you are experiencing? Write down the number. Do you think the number needs to go up or down?

2. Do your children truly know you, or is their knowledge only at a surface level? Have you told them stories about missteps you made when you were their age?

3. How often do you talk with your children at a deep level?

4. Are you showing, not just telling, your children how to be thoughtful and empathetic toward others?

5. Have you inadvertently been insensitive to the feelings of one of your children? Are you sure?

Action Ideas

1. When an appropriate setting presents itself, have each family member share an area of difficulty in their life for which they need their family's support and prayers. Be sure the parents share honestly as well, keeping in mind the children's maturity levels.

2. Go as a family to visit someone in the hospital. Be sure to coach the kids in advance on dos and don'ts. Go for lunch afterward and discuss your experience.

3. Encourage your children to celebrate other people's successes and happy occasions. Perhaps teach them to send messages to friends having birthdays or graduations.

4. Consider a family mission trip to spend time ministering to people less fortunate than you. This might be an international trip, or perhaps your church has local mission opportunities. Consider regularly volunteering as a family to care for the homeless or refugees.

5. Find someone in your church who is from another country or who has no family living nearby. Invite this person or family to spend a holiday with your family. Come up with a gift your family can give them.

6. When your family sees an ambulance driving with its siren on, have someone in your family offer a prayer for whoever is in distress.

Chapter Six

Resetting Your Default to Yes
Rebelling Against "No"

"I imagine that yes is the only living thing."
—*E. E. Cummings*

School on Fifth Avenue

When I (Carrie) was homeschooled, my mom and I sometimes fell behind with my schoolwork. We didn't procrastinate on purpose, but you know how life is—something invariably came up during the first six months of the school year.

I felt burdened by these delays. How could I enjoy my figure skating lessons, book club outings, youth group trips, or *American Idol* parties if I knew I had unfinished algebra problems? It is a testimony to my fortitude that I hid my torment so effectively it was hardly noticeable to those who knew me.

When spring arrived, the atmosphere in my home changed abruptly. Our house morphed from being a Carnival cruise ship to the battleship *Bismarck*. I studied industrial revolutions, world wars, politics, and tyrannical leaders (I'm not just referring to my mom's attempt to teach me long division before her morning cup of coffee).

We always ended a few credits short of our goal, so we had to get creative. My friends and I baked cookies—home economics! Double the recipe, and it's math too. Going to skating practice, or on a walk into town (or through the mall)? Physical education!⁵

---

5 My best friend and fellow homeschooler Olivia counted babysitting a six-month-old as weightlifting. I could only aspire to such levels of system-working mastery.

In 12th grade, I found myself in the same predicament as the previous five years: I was one class short. This time the stakes were higher, as I needed a particular number of credit hours to earn a high school diploma and commence university in the fall. Knowing my likelihood of passing physics was as good as my being a walk-on lineman for the Crimson Tide, I decided to go a different route: Drama 101.

One of the course requirements was to attend a live play. I had several options:

1. I could attend the children's choir Easter musical at my church armed with earplugs and pray the 13 young participants could complete the hour-long production without any mishaps involving bodily functions.

2. I could go to the local theater and see Oliver Twist. For the 15th time. By my sixth viewing I could quote every line, and my only excitement was predicting how far the middle-aged "Oliver" actor's hairline had receded since the previous year's production.

3. Or, there was a final option—the most brilliant and extravagant idea to traipse through my 17-year-old mind (and I was never small-minded when my ideas were bankrolled by my father): a Broadway musical in the Big Apple.

What could give me a better theatrical education than attending a musical on the most famed strip of real estate the arts has ever known? The only obstacle was convincing my dad to take me. Still, I was hopeful.

My oratorical performance would shame Cicero. I'd wait for the optimum moment to strike. Perhaps when his favorite hockey team, the Buffalo Sabres, was on a winning streak.[6] I'd make him a latte. I might even clean my room. Then I would discuss the benefits of the arts on young minds.

I'll bet Thomas Edison, Albert Einstein, and William Shakespeare's dads took them to see live plays as teenagers, and look at them now! Well, aside from being dead. It would be an educational experience, and nothing is more important than education.

My intentions were strictly scholastic. Tiffany and Company? Overpriced tin. Saks Fifth Avenue? Impractical and gaudy. The debauchery of the shopping scene was the furthest thing from my mind. And the idea of other sightseeing excursions was preposterous. Why would I *possibly* want to sit behind the south end of a dirty horse on a carriage ride through dreary Central Park? Lady Liberty? An overgrown lawn ornament. Eating in fashionable Manhattan restaurants? I hungered only for knowledge.

I would deplane at La Guardia, fulfill my school requirements, and hasten home to write my follow-up paper for Drama 101. Maybe we could swing by the Stock Exchange on the way to the airport and squeeze in a math lesson if we had extra time.

My face flushed as I finished my three-point, alliterated speech to my dad. To my utter shock, he didn't answer with a flat-out no. He had accumulated a nest egg of air miles and hotel points (the

6 On second thought, a snowball in Somalia had better odds.

silver lining in a busy travel schedule). We found an online deal for discounted tickets to the musical *Mary Poppins*.

My parents decided to turn the event into my graduation present, and my dad and I made a weekend of it. We spent two days touring the city and making some of the best father-daughter memories of my life. When we boarded the plane to return home, my feet ached, my eyelids sagged, and I felt like I'd just finished a marathon. But it was the most fun I'd ever had earning school credit. Years later, I've forgotten a lot of the dry biology lessons I endured at the kitchen table, but I often think back fondly on that trip.

We never did get around to seeing the Stock Exchange, but I enjoyed the carriage ride and shopping...

Confession of a Worn-Out Dad

When my kids were growing up, I (Richard) generally put in long days at the office. By the time I arrived home, I was exhausted. As I made a beeline for my recliner, my kids often buttonholed me. *"Dad! Can we go out to eat tonight? Mom says we have no food in the house!... Dad! Can you shoot baskets with me?...Dad! You said you would help me with my science project!...Dad! The Cavanaughs are going skiing this weekend, can we go, too?"*

On these occasions, I would inevitably feel a stirring from deep within my soul. Before I could stop myself, I would blurt out *"Noooooo!"* I batted away requests with the dexterity Roger Federer would handle a barrage of tennis balls. "We can't afford to go to Pizza Hut. What about frozen pizza? Oh, son, I'm really tired. Can we play basketball when I'm not so beat? Another science project??? Going skiing takes so much work. And money. Couldn't we do something a little less energetic, like watch skiing on TV?"

In my defense, most children have no idea how their parents pay for all of their recreational activities. Kids also tend to quickly scatter as soon as the party is over and it's time to clean up the mess. We parents can work up a long list of reasons to justify our "no." Our children usually focus on the *fun*, but not on the *work* involved. It's up to a responsible adult to factor in the logistics required for the escapades kids dream up.

In my home, I was that responsible adult. My wife wants to enjoy the journey no matter what the destination, so she was most often in the other camp. I was the lone holdout. My family began to assume that whatever fun idea emerged, I would douse it with the proficiency of a New York firefighter.

My sons banded together like a double helix. They even played the Bible card against me, lacing their arguments with Scripture. "What dad would give his son a snake when he asked for a fish? Or a stone instead of bread?" Although I admired their ability to cross-reference the book of Luke with the other synoptic gospels, I suspected they were beating me at my own game. But at least I understood their language. Lisa and Carrie bypassed the cerebral arguments and went straight for the heart. "You can't put a price on love." "You can always make more money but you can never relive a special family moment." I was flanked on both sides. What was I supposed to do?

It's in the Bible

The apostle Paul made a fascinating comment about Christian life. He claimed:

> For the Son of God, Jesus Christ, who was preached among you by us—by me, Silvanus, and Timothy—was not Yes and No, but in Him was Yes. For all the promises of God in Him are Yes, and in Him Amen, to the glory of God through us. (2 Corinthians 1:19-20)

Christian life is about freedom. The heavenly Father focuses on possibilities, not prohibitions. God has made numerous promises to His people, and when Christ is present, every promise is a resounding yes. Christianity is not frivolous, but neither is it the somber existence many people think it is.

With so many Christian homes characterized by negativism and restrictions, is it any wonder that the majority of children who grow up attending church head for the exits by the time they're young adults? They hear about "good tidings of great joy" at Christmas, but for the rest of the year, the message seems to be that when you follow Christ, you trade in gladness for rules. That shouldn't happen. Christian families ought to be characterized by joy.

What's a Parent to Do?

Conventional wisdom warns that children who always get what they ask for will become spoiled. It suggests that children might as well get used to being told "no" at a young age, because they'll be hearing that a lot for the rest of their life. Allegedly, John Rockefeller used to find out what his children wanted for Christmas just to make sure they didn't get it. He was determined that the children of the wealthiest man in the world would not grow up being coddled. As I (Richard) confessed, I wasn't always good at saying yes. I certainly didn't want to raise spoiled children, nor did I want them to assume they could get whatever they wanted, or that money grew on trees. So, I assumed I was being a good parent by regularly saying no. The problem was that too often I heard my children's *words,* but not their *heart.*

The Circus, Anyone?

Picture this: I drag myself in the door after a long trip, and my son Daniel greets me with, "Dad! Can we go to the circus?" I think to myself, *My kids always want to go somewhere expensive. I've barely walked in the door, and they're already flooding me with requests. They have no sense of fiscal responsibility. I have a lot to catch up on around the house. I don't have time to call the box office for tickets to the circus. I've been with people all week. The last thing I want is to go somewhere that's inundated with people, noises, clowns, and elephants...* So I blurt out, "No!"

By immediately going on the defensive, I make two mistakes. First, I hear my son's request, but I may totally miss his message. What he is really saying is, "I missed you, Dad! You've been gone all week. My friends all went to the circus with their dads. I could hardly wait until you got home so our family could do something together, too." My son missed me. He wants to spend time with me. If I'd had my act together, I'd have come bounding in the door waving circus tickets in my hand!

I'm not saying parents should wallow in a pool of self-reproach if our first instinct is to count the cost rather than readily agreeing to our child's suggestion (or making a promise we can't keep). But we should at least withhold our objections until we've considered the whole picture.

My second mistake is to focus on the problems instead of the possibilities. I automatically consider how late it is to get tickets for a show that evening. We haven't eaten dinner yet. Food prices at the circus are ridiculous. I don't know what commitments Lisa or the other children have for the evening, or if they even want to go to the circus (my wife dislikes big smelly animals). Because my mind focuses on obstacles and logistical details, what inevitably spews from my mouth is a resounding "no."

Mom: What child doesn't want to hear, "That's a great idea!" from Mom or Dad?

Now consider the same scenario, but with a different response:

I hug Daniel and tell him, "I *really* missed you! I want to spend time with you, too—how about we check with the family and make a plan?" He knows he's important to me and I'm open to his idea. We may discover that Carrie has a skating lesson that evening and Mike has a friend coming over. Mom has a casserole in the oven. But, we find tickets available for the next night, when everyone is available (and I've had time to catch my breath). For tonight, we settle on a cost-effective alternative—a fun table game, supplemented with an unhealthy platter of nachos. With some planning and effort, I can give Daniel a modified yes.

It's tempting for busy, tired, and broke parents to conclude that our children want the impossible. But often we fail to connect with their hearts, and as a result, we miss opportunities to make special memories with them. Maybe instead of the circus, we could go to a local baseball game or plan a hike for that weekend. Sometimes what kids ask really is impossible (Carrie sees no reason why we can't whip over to Paris for the long weekend). But most of the time, your children want time with you, a memory, and laughter. You ought to always be ready to provide those.

Mom: Having kids means you get another shot at doing all the fun things you wanted to do when you were young.

Challenge

Do your children live in a home of *no* or a home of *yes*? Becoming yes parents doesn't mean you surrender your leadership role to the kids or that you allow them to do whatever they want. It's not about relinquishing control or degenerating into anarchy; it's about channeling your resources in a more positive direction. How do you do this, especially if you are a task-oriented person? Two suggestions: First, strive to hear your child's heart. Second, think in terms of possibilities rather than impossibilities.

Growing up in a *Yes* Home

I (Carrie) was an imaginative child. I could look at a large cardboard box and see a bank. An old grey tracksuit was a mouse costume. A strip of colored paper was a princess crown.

My imagination led to many bright and often less-than-practical ideas. Some were obvious write-offs. I couldn't move to the Amazon rainforest and live like Tarzan (my mom asked who needed a jungle when my brothers' rooms contained as much wildlife as any rainforest ecosystem?). I couldn't become a poverty-stricken orphan and attend a British boarding school like Sara Crewe and the other heroines of my favorite books (though I occasionally heard my dad mutter that my brothers and I were driving him to the poorhouse). Other ideas were impossible for financial reasons.[7]

But when I came up with a feasible idea, I knew my parents would consider it.

As a child, I developed an obsession: pets. It took some asking, researching, and demonstrations of my mature sense of responsibility, but my mom ultimately agreed to get my brothers and me a fish. We named him Patch because of the orange splotch on his face. I loved him. I was devoted to him until my cousin Morgan decided my heathen fish needed some "Jesus" in his life and dropped a decorative stone church on top of him.

When she removed it, he floated belly up. "Don't worry," she said, "Your fish is just sleepin'." It was a deep sleep from which he never awakened. I can only hope he was converted before the lights went out.

The next time my dad went on a speaking trip, my mom took me to

Mom: Beautiful memories remain long after the bills are paid.

---

7 Though I still claim that adding an indoor hot tub and a swimming pool with a water slide to our house would have been a lucrative investment for my father and would have done wonders for my mother's health.

the pet store and we got a hamster. He was even better than Patch because he was furry and I could hold him. We conveniently forgot to tell my dad. When he arrived home from the airport after midnight, he flopped into bed and was almost asleep when he heard an odd creaking sound.

Bone tired, he lumbered out of bed and retraced his steps into the hall where he found the newest member of our family completing nocturnal exercises on his wheel.

Dad burst back into the bedroom and awakened my mother.

"WHAT, in the name of all that is good and sacred, is a RAT doing in our house?"

My mom yawned. "So you met Nibbles."

Dad was wary of leaving home again, but he needn't have worried. We knew better than to spring a pet on him again. We'd have to take a more direct approach next time.

When Nibbles finally nibbled his last, I decided it was time to move in for the kill. The ultimate goal. Every kid's dream. A puppy.

I borrowed some books about dogs from the library, and my mom and I spent ages researching to find the perfect pedigree. We located a Havanese breeder in a nearby city. Then we put together a 30-minute presentation, complete with handouts and flow charts on the benefits of owning a dog. It was so convincing, I marveled that I'd survived nine years of my life without a canine companion.

We took my dad to his favorite restaurant, and when his dessert came, I launched into my spiel. To my surprise, I was only halfway through point one when Dad agreed to consider it. He didn't even ask to see my comparative analysis on the correlation between pet ownership and low cholesterol. Though I suspect my speech wasn't the only reason he relented, I was happy to know he at least took my opinion seriously. We did end up getting a dog (who, at age 15, is becoming something of a death-defying anomaly).

Since then, I have presented hundreds of requests to my parents, from wanting to eat at a certain restaurant to asking to attend a particular school. They didn't always say yes. As the adults with more experience, they often could discern issues I hadn't considered. But I always knew that unless there was a compelling reason to say no, they would do their best to say yes.

Mom: Parents who never spoil their kids have unhappy kids.

Conclusion

Conventional wisdom encourages parents to ensure their children don't grow up to be spoiled. We're not advocating that you convey the message to your kids that you are a pushover who was placed on the earth to provide for their every whim. But the truth is that life can be difficult, and children only live in our home for a few, brief, memorable years. Therefore, parents ought to do whatever they can to facilitate joy and adventure in their family. And besides, when your children know you will say yes whenever you can, they also know you mean it when you say no.

Reflect and Respond

1. Did you grow up in a strict home or a lenient one? What bearing did your experience have on the way you treat your children?

2. Reflect on the last three things your children asked of you. What was your response? Take note of the next three requests and your response.

3. Are you known more for what you are for or what you are against?

Action Ideas

1. Consider whether your default answer as a parent is yes or no. Then sit down with each of your children and ask them the same question. Compare perspectives.

2. Have your children put various fun activities (that are doable) on separate sheets of paper. On a free family evening, have a child pull one of the slips of paper out of a hat. Agree that your family will do whatever the activity is that evening.

3. Reflect on an activity your children have asked to do that has seemed impossible. Quietly begin working on the logistics to make it happen. When you have the details worked out, find a creative way to announce the surprise to your family.

4. If you become aware of something fun your family would want to do, wait until one of your kids brings it up and be ready to say yes. You might have to drop some hints! Let it be "their idea."

Chapter Seven

Rules: Less Is More
Rebelling Against Pointless Prohibitions

"Rules are not necessarily sacred, principles are."
—Franklin D. Roosevelt

Touch Not the Plant in the Living Room

Mike, our firstborn, was our crash test dummy while Lisa and I (Richard) tried to figure out how to be parents. When he was born, I was a graduate student, and we were flat broke. Our apartment was so austere, it was difficult to tell if we had moved out or were moving in. It was childproof, as most barren rooms are. So, Mike was relatively free to roam about the tiny domicile and to play with whatever caught his fancy.

We set only one rule for Mike in his little universe. Besides the three of us, and the occasional cockroach, only one other living thing shared our apartment. That was a spindly dracaena plant, a gift from a well-intentioned friend. It was the sole object in our living room that was not secondhand. We instructed our wee lad that he was free to enjoy all the wonders of his small paradise, with one exception. He was not to touch the plant, or he would surely be punished. Naturally, he couldn't keep his pudgy little hands off of it. He loved to prune that shrub, and as fast as the leaves would grow back, he'd shred them off again.

The time came to draw a line. I squatted down so I was face to face with my little son. I explained to him, again, that he was not allowed to pluck from the tree. I asked if he understood what I was saying. He indicated that he did. I felt relieved that we'd finally come to a mutual understanding.

We'd hardly adjourned our meeting when I saw him furtively edge his way toward the plant. Reaching out his right hand, he defiantly touched it and then looked nervously at me. I came swooping down and took his right hand in mine so he could no longer touch the plant. Stubbornly sizing me up, he extended his left hand and pulled off a leaf. I seized his left hand in mine as well. Frustrated at this unpleasant turn of events, he began to back his diapered bottom into the forbidden foliage.

In hindsight (pardon the pun), I wonder if it would have been easier for all concerned if we had simply tossed the plant into the nearest dumpster and let our toddler roam free. But as dutiful parents, we wanted to teach him the importance of obedience. I know I was not the first, or last, parent to struggle with establishing reasonable household rules.

So What's the Problem?

How should parents apply rules in their home? We want to keep our young ones safe. And, as they grow older, we also want to protect them from being seduced by dangerous worldly pleasures. So how do we establish effective rules that will protect our children and prevent them from discarding their Christian values like yesterday's socks?

One approach is to adopt a *siege mentality*. We suspect the world is seeking to entrap and destroy our children, so we surround them with religious restrictions piled so high the evils of the world can't possibly reach them. We limit their social life to the church and its programs, with occasional supervised excursions to Bible camp. But the barricade plan could backfire. If they feel suffocated by sequestration, they might one day rebel, find ways to escape their safe cocoon, and end up in the grip of the enemy.

If our goal is to avoid the unpleasantness of a rebellion, we could opt for the *live and let live* approach. Let the kids make their own decisions and plot their own course through life. They will learn by trial and error how to navigate the hazards of the dangerous world we live in. That way they can't blame us for stifling their inner Zen. Besides, young people will inevitably sow their wild oats, won't they? Parents just have to hope they don't go too far. The risk of this strategy is that immature choices could cause harmful, even disastrous, life-long consequences.

A third option is the *emergency response* plan. We mind our own business until they get in trouble and then react accordingly. This leaves us free to pursue our own interests in the meantime, and we only have to rush in when necessary, hoses at the ready to douse the fire before it rages out of control. The reactionary approach allows parents to save their energy for when it's most needed.

Mom: Children who rebel are often the offspring of adults who didn't.

Obviously, each of the above strategies has drawbacks. Households must have rules, but how many? Which ones? How negotiable?

It's in the Bible

The Bible is often misrepresented as an ancient rulebook, a dusty old manual brimming with regulations and recriminations. In Western society, where personal freedom is the ultimate prize, many Americans (including Christians) see God's Word through a restrictive lens. We zoom in on the restraints and overlook the panoramic latitude our Creator has given us.

Take Adam and Eve. God told them, "Of every tree of the garden you may freely eat; but of the tree of the knowledge of good and evil you shall not eat, for in the day that you eat of it you shall surely die." (Genesis 2:16-17) The first couple was at liberty to do whatever they wanted, with only a single exception. They had an exquisite garden to explore, and an intimate relationship with their Creator to enjoy. Endless possibilities; one prohibition. No one could accuse God of being preoccupied with rules.

Even when you read the Old Testament Law that God gave to Moses, it is clear that the Lord was primarily concerned with *blessing* His people, rather than binding them. Unfortunately, people began to supplement God's laws so that relating to Him became a complicated and cumbersome process. That's why Jesus drove His enemies into hysteria when He dismissed their homespun rules and spoke out against oppressive legislation. Jesus was anything but a legalist.

Nevertheless, the Bible tells of parents who laid out some zany requirements. King Saul (not known as a Biblical paragon of stability) was at war with the Philistines. One day, he had a really bad idea. He decreed that no one could eat any food until the battle was over (1 Samuel 14:24-46). Of course, nothing whets the appetite like an all-day fight to the death, so Saul's soldiers grew faint. Still, they refused to eat for fear of the king's wrath. The best soldier on the field, Saul's son Jonathan, unknowingly broke the rule and helped himself to some honey. When the king found out, he prepared to enforce his statute and have his noble son slain. Only the intervention of his soldiers prevented the king from executing his own flesh and blood in order to enforce his foolish edict. Saul provides a classic example of a parent whose poorly conceived rule would have been disastrous had it been implemented.

The Bible focuses on *relationships*, not *rules*. It keeps injunctions to a minimum while promoting wholesome relationships and godly living. Families would do well to take heed of this.

What's a Parent to Do?

Every household must grapple with parameters. Several factors influence the boundaries parents establish, one of those being the nature of their children. Mike, Daniel, and Carrie were good-natured, happy kids. But they also had a stubborn side, as most thinking human beings do. Our family has always been intrigued by personality tests, and we have taken a number of different kinds (Myers-Briggs, for example). The results consistently proved what we already knew—we all have different quirks and character traits. So the way we operate as a family may differ from the way you do. But here are a few guidelines that we settled on:

1. *Challenge ridiculous rules.*

Ridiculous rules are everywhere. They make you shake your head in bewilderment that the rule-makers could have been serious. Allegedly, the following laws are still on the books:

- Chewing gum is illegal in Singapore, except for therapeutic reasons when prescribed by a doctor.

- In Thailand, it is illegal to step on currency because it is disrespectful of the monarch.

- In the United Kingdom it is illegal not to tell a taxman anything you don't want him to know, but it is legal not to tell him anything you don't mind him knowing (you may have to read that one twice).

- In Maine, it is illegal to leave Christmas decorations up after January 14th.[8]

- In Ohio, it's against the law to get a fish drunk.

- It is illegal to die in the British Parliament.

- In the tiny French village of Sarpourenx, dying without owning a plot in the local cemetery is "severely punished."

- In New Jersey, it's illegal to wear a bulletproof vest while committing a murder.

These rules are bizarre, aren't they? Yet, at one time, they made perfect sense to someone. That's the way it normally is with rules.

---

8 If you have neighbors who leave their inflatable reindeer lawn ornaments displayed until mid-April, this is one law you probably wish was enforced.

People don't set out to make rules that everyone will laugh at; it just happens. The result is that society ends up with meaningless, irrelevant regulations.

Strange Rules in My Friends' Homes

We weren't big on rules in our house when I (Carrie) was growing up, so I was naturally intrigued by the prohibitions my friends' parents established in their homes. Most of them I could understand, but every now and then I came across one that didn't make sense to me. Here are a few examples:

- No trick or treating, because participating in Halloween teaches bad values (but the girls were allowed to attend R-rated concerts).

- Every bite of food on your plate must be eaten (even when the food is a McDonald's cheeseburger and fries).

- Banned from watching *Harry Potter* or *Wizard of Oz* because of the witchcraft (*Lord of the Rings* was permissible, despite the wizardry, because it's a Christian allegory and practically the same as reading Habakkuk in King James English).

- Imperative for the boys to reply "Yes, Ma'am" when spoken to by a woman, to show respect for her (but no issues with dad and sons watching *James Bond* as 007 leapt in and out of danger while simultaneously leaping in and out of sexy women's beds).

- No piercings or non-natural colors of hair dye because that might send the wrong message (but the daughter was allowed to wear low-cut tops to school and date at 13).

Not all rules are bad, but parents must keep in mind that rules are merely a means to an end. They should be chosen and enforced with a long-term goal in mind and not merely to induce short-term compliance. Many parents want immediate results, so they establish rules that call for visible obedience in the current circumstance. They get the performance they want (their children do what they're told), so Mom and Dad mistakenly assume that all is well. Then they are shocked when their children go off to college and experiment with forbidden pleasures as soon as they escape the heavy-handed enforcers at home. Rather than instilling godly values in the children, the parents' rules only invite rebellion.

> *Mom: Short-sighted rules produce short-term results.*

It has been said that the period in which the Roman Empire imposed the greatest number of laws was when its society was most corrupt. The problem with rules is that they address symptoms, not root problems. They focus on outward behavior, not the heart. When parents pile rule upon rule on their children, they are essentially giving up on changing their children's hearts. Having numerous restrictions is a sign of defeated, directionless parenting, not good leadership.

2. Keep it simple.

During my (Carrie) brothers' and my teenage years, we didn't have a lot of hard and fast rules. In fact, our parents only had three. Because there were only three, we knew what they were and why they expected us to follow them. My mom and dad realized that most short-term punishments had short-term (if any) success. I had one friend who was repeatedly grounded for breaking the same rule. Obviously, grounding her wasn't working! My parents didn't threaten to take away our TV privileges, and none of us was ever grounded. They joked that if we were behaving badly enough to be confined to the house, the last thing they wanted was to be stuck under the same roof with us for two weeks.

My parents respected us and expected us to make the right choice. We knew that if we lost their trust, we would have a hard time earning it back. For us, that was the greatest deterrent they could have used.

Instead of informing us that we weren't allowed to drink alcohol or do drugs, they would point out people around us who did, and the real-life consequences that resulted. We talked about how one friend's drug experiment led to a fender bender. He tried (unsuccessfully) to lie his way out of any responsibility by claiming he was the victim of a hit-and-run. He ended up paying for some very expensive car repairs and having

> *Mom: Instead of telling your children they can't have something that's bad for them, explain why they don't want it in the first place.*

some extremely uncomfortable conversations with his parents and the police.

Another girl got pregnant when she was drunk. Her boyfriend ditched her faster than a New Year's resolution in February. Had she been sober, she wouldn't have gone to bed with him in the first place. She dropped out of school and gave up the sport she loved. She hurt her parents deeply and lost her reputation and self-respect.

By discussing these real-life examples with us, our parents didn't have to surround us with rules. We'd have been fools to go down those harmful paths. And we weren't fools.

3. Choose your rules carefully.

Parents should be careful that the rules they establish help their children rather than hinder them. Parents should focus less on rules and more on enabling their children to understand why something—like smoking—is a mistake. As a result, children will take ownership of the decision to choose health over cigarettes. When kids leave home, they will be free from their parents' rules, but the values they embrace at home will last a lifetime.

Lisa and I (Richard) fastidiously avoided setting ourselves up for pointless battles with our children. Every home needs rules. That's a given. However, parents must be sensitive to the fact that every rule invites conflict. If you establish a rule, be prepared for your child to push against it at some point. If you have 100 rules, expect a minimum of 100 violations. Consequently, the fewer the rules, the less chance of conflict with your kids! So, decide if all 100 of your rules are really worth the dissension they will inevitably invite.

We chose to focus on only three rules in our home. We aren't saying these should be your three rules, or even that you should only have three. But when we boiled down the goals Lisa and I (Richard) had for our children, we felt they could be accomplished by insisting on the following three behaviors:

Rule No. 1: Treat one another with respect. We had zero tolerance for family members disrespecting one another. We should add that we did enjoy playful teasing, but not hurtful insults. We would not abide one family member speaking badly about another, in their presence or otherwise. This also included parents. We might need to correct a child, but that didn't give us the right to demean them.

We put a great emphasis on this one. We didn't buy the myth that siblings are bound to argue. We acted on the assumption that siblings get along—that they enjoy one another's company, and that they are each other's greatest cheer-leader. That's not to say that our three cherubs never quarreled. But our kids' disagreements were rare, because they were taught to respect one another. The fact is most kids will live up to what is expected of them. Many parents simply don't expect enough.

I (Richard) remember when the family next door to us moved away. Our kids were disappointed because the family included two brothers near our boys' ages. They played with Mike and Daniel, but the

Mom: Children will live up to parents' expectations if the expectations are high enough.

best part was that they included Carrie in the fun, too. Maybe it was because they didn't have a sister, or maybe it was because she was used to hanging out with boys, so she knew how to behave when they found a snake in the yard. They were great neighbors, and we were sad to see them leave town. But to Carrie's delight, a new family moved in and they had a daughter exactly her age. We had the little girl over to play, but after she went home, Carrie declared she didn't want to play with this girl anymore. Lisa and I asked her why, and she responded, "She wanted to put a sign on my bedroom door that said, 'No boys allowed.' Why would she do that? They're not boys; they're my brothers."

We made no allowances for attitudes and behaviors that demeaned or divided our kids. They weren't simply brothers and sister; they were good friends.

Rule No. 2: Tell the truth. This second rule was a natural outcome of respecting one another. Again, it seems straightforward enough, but it's amazing how many families tolerate, and at times, tacitly encourage dishonesty. Some parents respond to their children's honesty by punishing them.

Brittany: "Mom, I'm sorry. I told you my friends and I were going to Rebecca's house last night. But after we left in the car, my friends all decided to go to the mall instead. I know I should have called you to come and get me, but the whole thing was so awkward..."

Mom: "Brittany Louise! I can't believe you did that! You are grounded for two weeks!" (As if Brittany is going to be honest with her mother next time!) Parents claim they want their children to tell the truth, but then they pounce on them when they do.

Lisa and I (Richard) repeatedly impressed on our children that we expected them to be honest with us. We respected their privacy as best we could. We didn't read their diaries or text messages, and we knocked on their bedroom door before entering. But we also let them know that parents have ways of knowing what their kids are doing (such as networking with other parents), so they may as well be upfront

Mom: Not all rules are golden.

with us. But deeper than that, we found that when we trusted our kids and treated them with grace when they had something to confess, our relationship was strengthened, not damaged.

Rules 1 and 2 ought to be in every parent's handbook. The next one is more subjective. But it's something we settled on in our home and it worked for us.

Rule No. 3: No dating until they were eighteen. This rule was an absolute in our home. No "boy has crush on girl in middle school" type of relationships; no "we're not allowed to date, but we're a couple on Facebook" relationships; no "special friendships" at school. No meant no when it came to dating.

As far as we knew, ours was the only family in our church that adhered strictly to this rule. Several fine Christian families kept their children out of the dating game until they were 16. We aren't here to judge what is best for other families or for your family. We settled on the age of 18 for several reasons:

- When teenagers date before they are 18, they rarely have the emotional maturity to sustain the relationship. For goodness' sake, 30-year-olds struggle to handle their relationships in a mature, healthy manner!

- Teenagers who date are far more likely to become sexually promiscuous and end up with regrets, including unwanted pregnancies or shame over how they conducted themselves with someone who did not ultimately become their spouse.

- We had watched documentaries suggesting that adolescents who date suffer higher than average rates of depression and suicide. This is in part because they are subject to two sets of emotions instead of one. If their girlfriend is upset, or depressed, or breaks up with them, then the boyfriend is brought low as well. We also knew of teenagers who committed suicide because their partner broke up with them.

- Teen couples tend to focus exclusively on their relationship and miss out on enriching experiences with friends, sports, and hobbies.

- Our dating rule freed our teenagers from the pressure of finding a date for every social event, because they weren't allowed to date anyway.

For these reasons, we drew a hard and fast line on this rule. The result? None of our children dated until after they turned 18. Believe it or not, never once did our children fight us on this one. They actually thanked us then, and they thank us now, for taking such a strong position that freed them to enjoy being young and unattached. We should add that Mike, Dan, and Carrie were all good-looking, popular kids. They could have dated at a younger age, had we allowed it. But we didn't. Now all three are adults. Mike, Daniel, and Carrie married amazing spouses.

Challenge

The problem with rules is that children can mindlessly conform to them without ever believing in them. Rules are never meant to take the place of your child's brain. In fact, your children *should push back* against rules that are bad or that don't make sense.

We often think compliant children are good children. If our son never breaks a rule, never argues, and never pushes back, we proudly declare he is a "good" boy. When a child continually digs in her heels, pushes back, and argues with per-

Mom: What you say to your child in anger alerts them to what you really think of them.

ceived injustice, we sigh and declare that this is our "problem" child.

On the contrary, children who readily acquiesce to their parents' wishes may easily succumb to their school friends' pressure as well. If you teach your child to mindlessly yield to your wishes, be aware that you may simply be raising a people-pleaser. Your child may be driven to make people happy, rather than to live by certain strong personal values.

We know a number of allegedly rebellious children who eventually became respected church leaders and ministers (some of them are our relatives). By the same token, we saw compliant children end up rejecting the beliefs and values that they grew up with. Adherence to your rules does not guarantee adoption of your values.

Parents can be arbitrary with their rules and punishments, resulting in confusing, contradictory messages for their children. For example, one mother wanted to punish her teenage daughter for missing curfew, so she restricted her from attending the youth worship service on Wednesday night at their church. Parents may take pride in the fact that they don't have a television in their house, but be oblivious to the fact that every day after school, their child heads over to a friend's house to watch television. Parents can put tremendous effort into rules that are in fact ineffective. That's why it's crucial to keep in mind the greater goal—character versus compliance.

> *Mom: Let your children challenge you: they may not be right, but at least they'll know they were heard.*

Conclusion

Some people assume they are good parents because they have developed an extensive list of household rules for their children to follow. The truth may be just the opposite. Perhaps you should celebrate when your child chafes against a questionable restriction and, instead, be concerned if one of your children is being too malleable.

Some families uphold unusual rules. Yet have you ever wondered what people would think if they heard a list of your family dos and don'ts? Would they pity your kids or wish they'd grown up in your home? House rules reflect a family's priorities. Parents must decide what they are aiming for with their children and then tailor the rules accordingly. Some restrictions take a lot of energy to enforce, but they focus on secondary issues. Having too many rules can distract you and your kids from what really matters. Rules should have a specific purpose. They ought to guide your children toward who they become, not merely restrict what they do.

Mom: Making your child act compliantly is far inferior to teaching them to live wisely.

Reflect and Respond

1. Make a list of the rules you have for your children. Evaluate them. Are they reasonable? Are they effective? Have your children embraced them or do they simply obey them?

2. What rule are you having the most difficulty enforcing? Why do you think that is?

3. List the methods you are currently using to enforce your rules. Do you think these are fair? Are they effective?

4. What are the top three goals you have for your children? Are your rules helping your children achieve those goals? Why or why not?

5. Do you currently have too many rules, not enough, or the right amount? What adjustments do you need to make?

Action Ideas

1. Ask your children to list your household rules. Take note of what they mention first. Consider what they leave out. Then discuss the rules as a family. Ask your children if the rules seem reasonable to them. Explain the rationale if you need to. Don't be defensive. Ask your children what appropriate consequences should be for infractions. If their suggestions are realistic, adopt them.

2. Plan a family game where you invent a set of crazy rules for a day. Perhaps you must open the refrigerator door with your left hand, or everyone must hop up and down twice when entering or leaving the kitchen. Then invent funny punishments for violators. Make sure parents are included!

3. Make a decorative sign (or have one made) listing your family's values, and display it in an appropriate place (rec room, entryway, etc.).

Chapter Eight
Well-Mannered Little Monsters
Rebelling Against Shallow Character

"Manners are the hypocrisy of a nation."
—Honore de Balzac

Emergency on Aisle Three

When my brothers and I (Carrie) were in our formative years, Mom's chief occupation was correcting our manners. She said it was for our own good, so we weren't mistaken for barnyard animals, but her constant reminders seemed downright oppressive to us. We weren't supposed to eat dirt, dog food, or gum from the sidewalk. Running around the house *au natural* after our bath was discouraged, especially when the blinds were open. She dissuaded us from riding down the hardwood staircase on our bed mattresses while singing "A Whole New World."

Her short-term goal was that we'd be house-trained by puberty. But she also had a Master Plan: by the time we reached marriageable age, we would be completely civilized and not frighten away potential spouses. Or more importantly, their mothers. She taught us how to use utensils properly, to say "thank you" when appropriate, and to avoid scratching certain parts of our anatomy in public.

Her diligence paid off—she claims that we three children were so angelic, it became common for strangers in restaurants or malls to approach her and Dad simply to commend them on their well-behaved kids. Though we might tussle and be rowdy at home, we knew better than to act out in public. Well, most of the time.

Mom tells me (and I believe her) that I was a particularly beautiful child, with big blue eyes and curly golden hair. She loved to dress me in flowery frocks with matching hair bows, frilly socks and shiny patent shoes, and then bask in the compliments from the public at large.

> Mom: "...the things that come out of the mouth come from the heart."
> Matthew 15:18

One such occasion stands out in her memory. I was two years old, and we were in the grocery store. As my mom scoured the produce aisle, I was sitting in the shopping cart behaving cutely (as was my custom). Apparently, my sweetness caught the eye of a teenage girl. "Oh, what a little doll!" the girl gushed. She smiled and waved at me, slowly drawing closer as she reached out to touch my curls. My mother beamed, the way she always did when someone admired her darling. The girl's face got closer and closer until it eclipsed everything else from my view.

Aggravated, I looked her in the eye and spat in her face.

So What's the Problem?

Parenting isn't as easy as it looks—and it doesn't look easy! With little or no formal training, moms and dads are expected to transform narcissistic mini-Neanderthals into civil, courteous human beings.

Babies enter the world entirely fixated on their own needs. Knowing nothing about etiquette, they care not a whit if Mommy is tired or Daddy is busy. They want their needs met... now! When they don't get what they want, they cry until they do, or until they forget what the fuss was all about. But by then, they want something else. If their high-pitched screams disrupt the tranquility of the night, or the ambience in a restaurant, or the mood of 200 passengers on an airplane, so be it.

Moreover, infants have no dignity—they belch, they scream at the top of their lungs, they don't cover their mouth when they sneeze, they put dead bugs in their mouth, and they allow noxious fluids to leak out of bodily orifices. It's nothing short of a miracle that these savages one day become nurturing schoolteachers, compassionate nurses, and distinguished dignitaries. If parents hope to achieve any success in domesticating their offspring, they must commence the enhancement process as soon as possible. Every parent who accomplishes the thankless task of civilizing a little human being is to be heartily commended.

Bless Their Hearts

We currently live in the Atlanta area. In many ways, life in Georgia is a throwback to the antebellum days of chivalry and decorum. Young boys and girls say, "Yes, Ma'am" and "No, Sir." Children reared in the South learn "thank you" and "yes, please" while still in the cradle, and they don't address adults by their first name alone. They refer to them as "Mr. Mark" or "Ms. Greta." We think it's charming when we hear kids greet us as 'Mr. Richard' and 'Ms. Carrie,' and who isn't putty in the hands of a six year old who

Mom: Etiquette should be like meringue on a pie: a sweet, fluffy, and attractive hint of the goodness that lies beneath.

already knows how to open the door for a lady? But, as many of us have learned, that is only half the battle. The most decorous young person in the room is not necessarily the most thoughtful.

Don't Just Say Something, Do Something!

Say two young men, Nathan and Joe, are sitting at your dinner table. After the meal, Nathan says, "Well now, Ma'am, I believe that was the finest meal I've eaten in days. Just like my mama makes. God bless her. I surely do thank you. Please excuse me." He exits the room. Joe says, "Thanks for dinner." He picks up his plate and cup, as well as the dirty dishes Nathan left behind, carries them over to the dishwasher, then exits the room. Which guy would you rather have as a guest? Better still if a third young man were there, and the only thing that came out of his mouth was "Can I help with dishes?" You get the point. Nathan would do well to be a little less pedantic and a little more pragmatic.

Mom: Stop flattering me and pick up a dishcloth!

It's not enough to teach your children to *say* nice things. You want them to develop into thoughtful people who *do* nice things.

What's a Parent to Do?

When I (Carrie) was little, our family was often invited to other people's homes for meals or dessert. Dad was a pastor and we were poor, so receiving invitations that involved being fed was always exciting. We knew the food would be delicious, and, if the host family had children, there would be toys. We could hardly wait!

However, first we had to endure Dad's customary speech as we drove to our host's house. As soon as our seat belts were buckled, he would clear his throat and begin the Etiquette Catechism. The lesson would continue until we pulled into the host's driveway.

"Now kids, I trust you to behave, but it never hurts to go through some guidelines ahead of time," he would say (every time). He sometimes adopted a Q and A format, I guess to better engage us in the learning process.

Guideline One:

Dad: "Why did we make such an effort to arrive on time?"

Us: "Arriving late means we think our time is more valuable than theirs."

Guideline Two:

Dad: "When is it appropriate to interrupt the adults' conversation?"

Us: "If we are projectile vomiting, bleeding profusely, or combusting into flame."

Dad: "And?"

Us: "If it doesn't appear to be subsiding."

Guideline Three:

Dad: "What if you don't like the food they serve?"

Us: "We eat it, even if it's boiled frog toes with eyeball dressing."

Guideline Four:

Dad: "What is even better than saying, 'Thank you for letting us play with your toys?'"

Us: "Cleaning up before we leave."

Guideline Five: (this one was a trick question)

Dad: "What is a polite way to indicate you are bored and want to go home?"

Us: "There is no polite way. If we say we are bored and want to go home, we are in huge trouble when we *get* home."

Dad's drill must have worked, because we received numerous repeat invitations.

I (Richard) wanted to instill manners into our children, so Lisa and I did direct them to say "please," "thank you," and "excuse me." But we also tried to help them understand that their behavior spoke louder than their words.

For every one of the guidelines Carrie mentioned, I could tell a story of why we made it one of our expectations. For example, I once traveled to a different state for a speaking engagement. The host pastor invited me to his house for a meal. The pastor had some important matters he wanted to discuss with me. However, his eight-year-old son would not leave us alone. The boy interrupted us every few minutes with a loud *"Excuse me!"* Then he would effuse about something he had just seen on television. His frequent interjections were inappropriate, unnecessary, and frankly, annoying. But whenever the boy would butt in, his father would smile and commend him for remembering to say "excuse me." The boy was learning how to be rude, politely. His words may have been respectful, but his actions were self-centered and inconsiderate.

It's in the Bible

Jesus was not fooled by pretentious behavior. He sternly reprimanded the scribes and legalistic Pharisees for calling attention to their pious decorum while, at the same time, harboring deceit and judgment in their hearts: *"Even so you also outwardly appear righteous to men, but inside you are full of hypocrisy and lawlessness."* (Matthew 23:28) Jesus despised the very thing the religious leaders were proud of—their public persona.

If we transferred the above scenario into today's religious community, what would it look like? Perhaps Jesus would rebuke the impeccably coifed choir members for huddling together on the soprano side to gossip about one of the altos, or He would call out the gentlemanly deacon who stands up whenever a lady enters the room, but demeans his wife at home.

Mom: In our attempt to charm the world with our mannerly children, let's be careful we don't produce manipulative little monsters.

Certainly, children must learn to behave respectably, but parents should aim deeper than that. We must keep in mind that Jesus was not bashing the religious elite for being devout—He was targeting their hypocrisy. He admonished them because they *pretended to be something they were not.* We would do well to spend more effort teaching our children about love and kindness and less time coaxing Oscar-worthy performances from them when we have company over for dinner.

Meticulous but Malignant

Josef Mengele was a young German with flawless manners. His mother, though not overly affectionate, instilled in Josef and his brothers the importance of treating their parents with respect and practicing the faith of the church. Like most young German citizens, he had a love of country and he valued tradition.

As a student, Mengele was known for being punctual, hard-working, and well-behaved. Many of his teachers commended him for these qualities. He was not the top student in his class, but his charm and social skills earned him favor with his classmates.

Mom: It's enviable to teach your child etiquette, but it's essential to build their character.

As an adult, Mengele was exceedingly conscious of his personal grooming. Naturally a handsome man, Josef made it a point always to look his best. He never went to work without every hair in place, and his uniform (always the most formal option) carefully laundered and pressed. He washed his hands frequently and thoroughly with perfumed soap. He was a cultured man. He enjoyed opera music—and often hummed to himself the tunes of his favorite composer, Richard Wagner. He valued education and earned doctorates in both anthropology and medicine. Because of his warm smile and charisma, people who met him immediately liked him.

The problem was that Josef Mengele was an extraordinarily cruel, heartless person.

He became deeply involved in the Holocaust atrocities perpetrated during World War Two and was responsible for the death of thousands of men, women, and children. He used his medical knowledge to conduct inhumane experiments on his victims—often inflicting devilish torture on people to see how much the human body could endure. Some of his favorite research involved studying the genetics of twins. It is estimated that he "treated" more than 3,000 twins. Few survived.

Even more disturbing, most of his coworkers were so disgusted by the brutality they were committing, they turned up for duty under the influence of mind-numbing substances such as alcohol, but Josef remained sober and alert. He thoroughly enjoyed his work.

Nicknamed the "Angel of Death, " he is ranked among the most evil men of all time. Though outwardly polished, his character was seriously flawed. His master, Adolf Hitler, was a teetotaler, non-smoking vegetarian who abhorred the thought of causing harm to animals. Clearly, a manicured, pleasant outward appearance can cover an evil, dark soul.

Mom: There's no excuse for selfishness. Anyone, young or old, bright or slow-witted, beautiful or plain, rich or poor, can be a thoughtful person by following one simple rule. It's found in Luke 6:31.

Birthday Brats

Nothing brings out the less-noble nature of children more than their own birthday party. I (Carrie) had several classmates in elementary school who used their birthday party as a blatant excuse for an extended Me-Fest. The formalities began weeks in advance. First they leveraged the invitation as a power tool on the playground: "If you don't play the game I want to play, I won't invite you to my birthday party." They made Lady Astor seem inclusive by comparison. They dropped enormous hints about potentially acceptable gifts, and waxed eloquent about the work that had already begun on cake construction.

On the big day, they seized the stage and monopolized everyone's attention. After all, they were the celebrity. The focus of the extravaganza was always on the birthday girl. We watched her open presents; we ate what she liked; we gave her the place of honor and played her favorite games. I remember at age seven, I attended one party where we played musical chairs.[9] The catch was that we all had to try to lose so the birthday girl could win, since it was "her day." What fun!

Some parents want to avoid the above situation, so they choose to forego the party altogether. Instead, they celebrate quietly as a family and perhaps with the money they save, buy a special gift.

> *Mom: The sign of a successful party is if the guests are glad they came.*

My mom would have none of that. She was a party animal who wouldn't dream of passing up an opportunity to haul out the streamers and balloons. My mother could have made a career out of throwing parties. She used to say party throwing was her spiritual gift. As a result, my parties were always elaborate (more on that in Chapter 10). Here's how she managed to make a big deal about my birthday parties without making me think I was a big deal.

She and Dad made it clear that my birthday party was a chance to celebrate "me," but it was also our family's job to see that my friends had fun. Every year as we planned my party, I was reminded

9 I might add that nothing gives a child heart palpitations quite like the stress of musical chairs. To this day I feel lightheaded when the game is even mentioned...

that I was to be a hostess, not the star of the show. For that reason, we planned games and activities my friends would enjoy. We made it a tradition to take a picture of each guest that we sent home with them. We had some seriously fabulous goodie bags. The party was in my honor, but it wasn't all about me.

When my brothers and I became adults and approached marriage, we found that the same principles of birthday party etiquette applied to weddings.

When I (Carrie) got engaged, my fiancé and I were excited to start planning the wedding, but our main goal (besides marrying each other) was that our families and friends enjoy themselves and take away great memories of our special day. We'd attended dozens of weddings together, so when the time came to plan our own nuptials we figured, how hard can it be?

We started reading wedding magazines and checking websites like Pinterest and The Knot. Sam even watched *27 Dresses* with me. Good grief. We realized that NASA launches are less complicated than wedding planning.

The term "Bridezilla" is infamous for a reason. People often talk about the wedding as "the bride's day." But it really isn't, or at least it shouldn't be. It's a special commitment between a couple and God, and it's also a time to show gratitude toward the people who invested in your life—including the groom! Many

Mom: Only one thing is more annoying than a little girl who thinks the world revolves around her. That's a grown woman who thinks the same thing.

brides (and sadly, their mothers) become so fixated on the flower arrangements, cake decorations, and ice sculptures that, though their wedding might be aesthetically pleasing, it is a miserable ex-

Mom: Strive to be kind in your heart and both your words and your actions will respond accordingly.

perience for the guests. One girl I know became so demanding during the wedding process that when she returned from her honeymoon, her own sister wouldn't speak to her. Any event with those results, no matter how beautiful the wedding dress, has missed the mark.

The reason young women become "Bridezillas" is because they never learned to be thoughtful people when they were young. If a child can learn to be a gracious host at her birthday party, odds are good she'll also be charming at her wedding one day.

Dad's Teaching Boys About Girls

Here's an idea. If you want to be counter-cultural today, teach your children that boys and girls are different. And if you really want to go out on the edge, teach them they should be treated differently!

Children are being inundated with confusing messages (to say the least) about how men should treat women. Pornography spews out of every crevice in society portraying women as mere objects for men's pleasure. There are religions that teach that women should be completely subjugated to men. And now, society appears increasingly confused about what constitutes a man or woman in the first place, as demonstrated by a popular magazine naming a biological man as its "woman of the year." In such a society, it's not surprising that many young men are inept at best and predatory at worst, in their relationships with women.

I (Richard) remember having a talk with my two sons when they were teenagers. They pointed out that I treated Carrie differently than I treated them. I admitted they were correct, but I explained that girls were wired entirely differently than boys. I told them that numerous reliable studies demonstrated that a girl's sense of self-worth stemmed largely from how her father treated her as she was growing up. Girls who were abused or disrespected often grew up with a low view of themselves. Girls whose dads cherished them and treated them with kindness came to believe they were a person of value who ought to be respected by others. I assured my sons that while my love for all three kids was equal, the way I expressed it would be different.

I told my boys that as best as I could, I had determined to treasure their sister so she grew up with a healthy sense of self-esteem and dignity. I encouraged them to help Carrie by treating her like a lady. I instructed them never to speak crudely around her or to make disparaging comments about her appearance, even in jest. I told them it was tough growing up as a young lady when society depicted girls as sexual objects evaluated solely by their physical appearance. Mike and Daniel agreed I was on to something. They said they would do their part for their sister as well. Over the years I was pleased to see my boys watch out for Carrie's safety and well-being. They even corrected their friends if they thought Carrie was being treated disrespectfully. Then I reminded them that every young girl they encountered was someone's sister.

Conclusion

Having well-mannered children is a worthy goal, but it is not the most important objective. Some of the brattiest kids you'll ever have the misfortune to meet have *please* and *thank you* down to a science. They have learned that those magic words get them what they want. Flattering words mean little if they flow from a selfish, deceitful heart. Don't be content when your children look great on the outside. Relentlessly work to make them beautiful on the inside, too.

Reflect and Respond

1. Do your children (even if they are adults) know the difference between etiquette and empathy?

2. Jot down some of the expectations you have for your children (and yourself) when you are guests in someone's home. Are you a pleasure to host, or are you the guests from you-know-where?

3. Write down one way your family could improve as it hosts others in your home. Talk about it as a family. Make plans to practice your new plan soon.

4. Consider birthday parties (and other celebrations) at your house. Do they encourage thoughtfulness for others or self-centeredness? What adjustments might you need to make?

5. How are you teaching your children to express gratitude, not just verbally but in other creative ways?

6. Remember, children learn by watching their parents. Consider your own behavior. Are you a phony? Do you

project a considerate image at church or in public, but lose your manners at the door when you get home?

7. How do you and your spouse treat one another? Could you make some improvements?

Action Ideas

1. As a family, discuss how you could encourage another family by having them over to your house for dinner or dessert. Brainstorm ways each family member could help to make the experience a pleasant one. Then invite the family over and try it. Don't forget to debrief afterward.

2. Brainstorm with your children several ways your family can be gracious houseguests. Write down what you came up with and pull out the list the next time you are invited out.

3. Make one evening at your house all about manners. Have every family member contribute one manner that they think is important for every family member to do. Compile a list and read it. For the rest of the evening, have everyone go out of their way to exaggerate those particular manners. Make a game of it. While it will be fun at the time, it will also reinforce that manner for the future.

4. At the dinner table one evening, take a moment to go around the table and have everyone mention something thoughtful that each family member does or has done. This will not only uplift each person, but will also reinforce the importance of being thoughtful toward others.

Chapter Nine

Yes, Kids, Life IS a Party!
Rebelling Against Joyless Living

"Home should be the treasure chest of living."
—Le Corbusier

My Mother Taught Me to Sleep Around

I (Carrie) got a Winnie the Pooh tent for my sixth birthday. It was just big enough to fit a child-sized sleeping bag comfortably. I decided that instead of snoozing in my bed with its soft mattress and fluffy comforter, I would spend the night on the floor inside my adorable, new-plastic-smelling Winnie the Pooh tent. And, of course, I asked my mom to sleep in there with me since I was too afraid of Heffalumps and Woozles to go it alone.

My mom, who has odd nocturnal preferences herself, once confessed it was her lifelong dream to sleep in a bathtub. She quickly agreed. We made a party out of it, complete with a "midnight snack" (which she later told me we ate at 8:30).

It was bliss.

From then on, my mom, brothers, and I made a game of sleeping in as many locations in our home as possible, usually when my dad was away on business trips. (After spending half his nights in hotel rooms, the idea of bunking down anywhere but his own king-sized bed was as appealing as a rendezvous with Bozo the clown in a deserted alley at midnight.)

The rest of us slept in our basement, on the hide-a-bed in the living room, in a fort under the Ping Pong table, and my uncle's tent trailer that we parked in our driveway. My dad got a garden shed a few years later, which I converted into a playhouse. At intervals, it became an orphanage, clubhouse, Hollywood studio, and castle. My mom and I dragged a futon into it along with some foams and sleeping bags so we could have sleepovers. The memories we made there were glorious. (Not including, of course, the morning when we were abruptly awakened by the sounds of a construction crew working on the house next to ours. Stranded in mismatching pajamas without a brush or makeup, my mom refused to leave the shed until the crew dispersed for lunch. She said slow and torturous starvation was more appealing than emerging into the light of day looking like she did.)

> Mom: If you want to know what's going on in your child's head, enter their world.

We slept in the shed off and on until the day we discovered a dead mouse under the futon. My mom and I ran to the house, dead-bolted the door, and refused to enter the shed ever again. My dad was happy since he was finally able to store the lawnmower and shovels in it, which was the reason he bought it in the first place.

> Mom: Go on some adventures with your children. They will never forget them!

I will be eternally grateful to my mother for teaching me to enjoy life to the fullest, in every circumstance.

So What's the Problem?

Conventional wisdom claims that parents are responsible for helping their children grow up into mature, self-sufficient adults. The thought of a middle-aged son or daughter still living at home, unemployed, single, and unmotivated, compels parents to do everything possible to ensure their children eventually become mature, autonomous adults. Fair enough. But in their zeal to instill responsible character traits into their kids, such as a strong work ethic and dependability, parents can end up with negative results they didn't expect. Tactics meant to equip a child for adulthood sometimes have harmful side effects. For example, kids who are pushed to overachieve may learn to work hard, but they may also come to believe that life is all work and no play. Parents who assume they are preparing their children for life by always pushing them to work hard may actually be causing more harm than good.

Below are five practices parents commonly embrace with the assumption that they yield desirable results.

+ Children are given numerous chores to do every day after school and on Saturdays so they learn to "pull their weight."

– But they have little time for hobbies or social activities.

+ Parents encourage their children to apply for part-time jobs as soon as they are old enough. This teaches them to punch a time clock and to manage their money.

– However, their job also prevents them from playing team sports, going on extended vacations with the family, and attending summer camp.

+ Parents equate inactivity with laziness, so whenever they catch their children "hanging out" at home, they give them another job to do. This teaches the children to be (or at least appear to be) productive.

    – But it also motivates them to spend their free time at their friends' houses.

+ Children have to learn that money doesn't grow on trees, so parents make their kids work for an allowance and use their own earnings to pay their expenses. This helps their children grasp the truth that nothing in life is free.

    – But it also teaches them to obsess about money at a young age.

+ Parents believe children don't appreciate college if they don't pay for it themselves. So they require their teenager to get a job after they graduate from high school so they can save enough money to further their education. This teaches them that a college education is valuable (and expensive).

    – But it also means some bright, high-potential young adults will never make it to university.

A National Work Ethic

Historians have argued that America's eventual greatness stemmed in large part from its Protestant work ethic. The Puritans who immigrated to North America believed that hard work honored their Creator (it also made many of them rich). This outlook on life resulted in the United States becoming the most wealthy and powerful nation on earth. However, it also birthed an exhausted populace with all manner of stress-related illnesses and the least amount of vacation time in the Western world. Over the years, America developed a culture that venerates the ant and despises the sloth. Work hard, and you are admired. Appear not to work hard, and your character is called into question.

Here's an experiment. Ask half a dozen friends this question: "How are you doing?" Then listen to their responses. More than likely, you will hear answers such as: "Busy as ever!" "Swamped!" "Hanging in there!" "Life is pretty crazy right now." "As good as can be expected." The thing is, these aren't viewed as unhealthy responses. America is a country where being a workaholic earns a badge of honor.

Then, when it's your turn, say something like, "Life is wonderful! Yesterday I slept in and just lay in bed listening to the birds singing outside. Then I went for a walk and counted the number of different flowers I saw along the path. After that I spent some quality time with a dear friend. I feel great!" Before you confess that you made all that up, take note of the expression on your listener's face (and assure them they don't need to call 911).

Our culture values activity and, more specifically, productivity. Christians often rank among the worst offenders—oh, how we love to remind ourselves that even Adam had to work, caring for the animals in Eden. Pastors tell their people they'd rather "burn out than rust out" and you'll have to pry their withered knuckles off the pulpit to put them in their coffin. The "soft" activities, such as hobbies, rest, and relationships, are considered luxuries to be enjoyed if and when all the work is finished. We program the next generation to believe that life is work and often drudgery. People enter the workforce with goals of toiling until retirement, hoping to live long enough to enjoy what remains of their life.

Religion Is Work, Too

There is another troubling aspect to this issue. Some parents unwittingly treat their faith the same way they view their job—as an obligation. Parents who try to indoctrinate their children with Christianity in the same way they strong-arm their kids into doing their chores should not be surprised when they meet with resistance. "Go to school, get a job, eat your veggies, get annual dentist cleanings, read your Bible, and go to church." How appealing is that to a child, or a teenager, or an adult for that matter? We may as well say, "Who wants to get up early on Sunday morning, put on itchy clothes and drive to church rather than sleep in, stay in their PJs, and enjoy a leisurely breakfast? We are Christians and we *always* do the right thing! We may be miserable and cranky, but we'll be counted among the faithful."

Mom: The reason many young adults are leaving the church is not because of hypocrites in the church, but because of joyless Christians in their home.

What we're getting at is this: many people go through religious rituals each week treating their Christianity like another task. The consequence of this attitude is predictably dismal—children who are dragged to worship services and Bible studies each week as a duty are growing up and deserting the church in droves. The good news is, it doesn't have to be that way.

I (Richard) have counseled hundreds of parents who were distraught that their children had walked away from their faith. These sincere folks dutifully carted their children off to every church program. They conducted family devotions. They stressed weekly involvement in Bible study. These parents also warned their children about the innumerable evils the world would tempt them with. Nevertheless, their children ignored their guidance and abandoned the church. The parents have no idea what went wrong.

The problem usually isn't the church—it's often the parents, or more specifically, the type of home the parents create for their children. Whether you agree with that conclusion or not, please hear us out on this one.

It's in the Bible

Lazarus, Mary, and Martha were Jesus' friends. Martha was hosting Jesus and His disciples in her home one day when something unexpected happened. Mary joined the men instead of helping in the kitchen.

While Mary sat mesmerized by the Messiah's teaching, her sister had a meltdown. It takes a lot of work to feed a houseful of hungry men. Mary was mingling with the guests while Martha frantically prepared lunch. Luke's account of the incident reads, "But Martha was distracted with much serving." (Luke 10:40) It must have been extremely awkward when Martha implored Jesus to make Mary help her with the chores. But, as He so often did, the Lord zeroed in on the real problem. He told Martha to stop fixating on the food and to focus on her friends.

Martha fell victim to a common mistake that has tripped up numerous hosts and hostesses—she became so stressed by the task of feeding her guests that she didn't enjoy their company. When that happens, the party is a flop. No one on the *planet* had a greater potential for joy than Martha did that day. She had the Son of God in her living room! The twelve apostles had come. Her beloved brother and sister were present. But she was so task-oriented, she almost ruined the experience.

Martha was more than likely the older sister. Her thought process may have gone something like this: "It's fine to have fun now and then, but life isn't a party. Someone has to bake the cookies and make the coffee. If everyone pitches in and gets the work done, then we can all have fun." Martha's problem was that by the time her work was done, the party would be over and the guests would have gone home.

What's a Parent to Do?

How can you rear your children so they don't embrace the harmful norms of our culture? How can you help them learn to enjoy life while simultaneously growing in their relationship with God? Let's first look at helping your family enjoy life in general. Then we'll consider ways you can encourage your children to *enjoy* their walk with God.

Enjoying the Journey

In many modern cultures (including America), adults teach children to focus on the destination at the expense of enjoying the journey. People strive to pay their mortgage, build their retirement, get through the workweek until Friday, and hang in there until their annual vacation. Children learn the benefits of delayed gratification (and there are benefits), but they are not necessarily encouraged to savor the moment.

Stressed in the Alps

I (Carrie) had an eye-opening experience one summer that made me view North American culture in a new light. My fiancé and I accompanied my parents on a "working" trip that took us through Switzerland, Germany, and Austria.[10] We ate in a number of restaurants. The food was delicious, but one thing drove us to distraction—it took hours to eat a meal! We waited to be seated, waited to be served, waited for our water, waited for our entrée, waited for our dessert (we felt obliged to always have dessert so we didn't offend the locals), then waited endlessly for the bill. Our servers were never in a hurry. At first we chalked it up to poor service, but after patronizing several different cafés, we noticed it was the same everywhere. One waiter was so reluctant to bring us the check that my dad finally cornered him in the kitchen so we could pay and still squeeze some more sightseeing into our day. We wondered how any eating establishment could survive without quickly herding their customers in and out the door.

Then, we began to observe the other customers. They seemed to be having a great time. They weren't hurriedly wolfing down their food. After the meal, they tarried at their table chatting with their companions. They lingered over their coffee (well, for some it wasn't just coffee). Spending time together at the restaurant was their desti-

10 My dad worked; the rest of us went along to make sure he wasn't lonely.

nation! It wasn't hard to pick out the other Americans in the room. They were the harried-looking ones who kept impatiently glancing at their watches while scanning the room for anyone in black pants and a white shirt.

There we were in a beautiful country, in the company of people we loved dearly, yet we struggled to enjoy the experience. Why? Because it took too much time. Who said dinner should only last an hour? Why would we get frustrated with a proprietor who didn't whisk away the dishes and send us packing as soon as we set down our fork? We had become victims of our North American culture.

Here are a few ways you can help your family resist the cultural pressures that shape the way you view your time and life:

1. Model a healthy lifestyle for your children.

Children do what they see far more often than what they are told. It is fine for you to instruct your children to live healthy lives, but you need to demonstrate what that looks like. The truth is, parents who constantly feel stressed will have offspring who suffer from stress as well. Obese parents often produce obese offspring. Physically fit parents tend to rear physically fit kids. I (Richard) have spoken with several workaholic businesspeople who confessed that their parents constantly worried about money. As a result, their children grew up anxious to achieve financial security. Parents must recognize that their example will exert enormous influence on their children.

Chill Out!

By now you know that relaxing has not always been my (Richard) strong suit as a parent, to put it mildly. I've taken various personality tests, and all of them place me solidly in the task-driven category. For years, I judged the success of my day or week or trip or year (or vacation) based on how "productive" I had been. I travel a great deal, so when I am at home, I always have an endless list of tasks. Therefore, if I ever find myself at home during the evening or on a weekend, I feel that I should be at my desk working. Carrie still remembers the first time she saw me sitting in our living room in the evening without a work-related book or laptop in front of me. She was a teenager. But do you know what happened? All of my children developed over-the-top busy schedules as young adults. It has not been easy helping my children overcome the unhealthy habits they formed while emulating me.

I (Richard) had a conversation with my mother a couple of years ago. She said she and my dad had been extremely busy of late, but they were "hanging in there." She expressed concern that she might not make her Platinum Elite frequent flyer status with Delta Airlines that year (which requires a minimum of 75,000 miles flown during the year) because she had to cancel a trip when my dad had quadruple bypass surgery. She was 75. He was 78. I know where I get my tendencies.

When I cued in to my workaholic tendencies, I tried to model a gentler life pace for my children, then teenagers. For one, I committed that, regardless of how busy I was, I would always stop what I was doing and give them my full attention if they came into my home office while I was working. They appreciated it, and they did not abuse the privilege by constantly pestering me.

Lisa and I have also built some relaxing habits into our lives, such as watching classic TV episodes together. Having grown up in

Canada, our childhood was deprived of some of the best American shows, like *The Andy Griffith Show*. We also take walks. More recently, I've begun reading fiction before I go to bed, rather than staying up late every night desperately trying to clean out my inbox.

About a year ago, Lisa and I made some big changes for the better in our eating habits. We lost weight and gained energy. All of our adult children saw the results and followed suit. None of them needed to drop more than a few pounds, but they wanted to join us in getting healthier. Like I said, I'm not an expert in this area, but I have come to see that I owe it to my kids to keep trying until I get it right.

2. Protect your children from harried living.

Society urges parents to enroll their children in a wide variety of enriching activities, including sports, music, recreation, clubs, and church programs. The reasoning is that children need numerous opportunities to develop skills and interests. The result of our love affair with busyness is that school-age children have schedules brimming with homework, tutoring sessions, Little League, music lessons, church events, and much more.

Parents must consider the benefit of each activity within the greater context of their child's health and well-being. There are many worthy pursuits, but they don't all have to be undertaken at once (or ever). Some wise parents limit their child to one extra-curricular activity per semester, and that's commendable. Along with that, we must also watch for other more subtle or "unscheduled" responsibilities our children take on. For example, if your daughter enjoys babysitting for the neighbors and makes a little spending money at the same time, that's great. But if it becomes a three-times-per-week activity and eats up all of her spare time, it should be reexamined.

Stop Studying and PLAY!

I (Carrie) am a nerd when it comes to academics. My cousin Anita swears J.K. Rowling based the *Harry Potter* character Hermione Granger on me. Because good grades have always been important to me, I put a lot of pressure on myself to do well at school. One day when I was in third grade, I came home from school in tears. My mother feared that a bully must have cornered me at recess, or that the class' pet hedgehog had gone to the great hedge in the sky. But no, it had been much worse than that. Whimpering and drawing ragged breaths, I handed her the crumpled, soggy piece of paper that I had balled up in my fist.

It was a math test with a B+ scrawled across the left corner.

"I practically failed!" I moaned.

That was the same year my teacher moved my desk close to hers so she could share her stress ball with me—the one she kept handy for times when the "difficult" students annoyed her to the breaking point.

As I progressed through school and my workload became increasingly difficult, I spent more time hitting the books. As a college student, it wasn't unusual for me to use the majority of my free time working on papers or studying for tests.

One day, I returned home after a full day of classes and a forty-minute commute, bleary-eyed and pale. I immediately settled into my chair to begin studying for my upcoming biology midterm. After a few minutes of reading about the respiratory system, I was startled when the door to my room burst open and my mom came bustling in.

"Carrie, I command you to stop studying this minute and go have fun!"

I gaped at her in shock while she threatened to hide my textbooks for a week if I didn't listen to her. I spent the rest of the evening reading for pleasure, jogging in the fresh air, and watching reruns of *Full House* with my brother. I felt relaxed and refreshed. All I needed was permission from my parents that it was okay to have downtime now and then.

I ended up getting an A on the Biology test, even without the extra couple hours of studying.

3. Strive to build fun into your family.

Some families simply aren't much fun. That's the sad truth. It's not necessarily their fault. They may have descended from a long line of boring families. If this happens to be your sad lot, we encourage you to break the dreary cycle as soon as possible.

I (Carrie) spent a lot of time at friends' houses over the years. Some homes were always fun places to hang out. You could hear laughter erupting from different rooms. The family would be enjoying making a meal together, or watching a favorite television show, or playing a game. The parents had funny stories to tell about recent misadventures. When I think of those families, even years later, I still associate pleasant feelings with them.

Other homes, however, were more like a cross between a funeral home and *The Hunger Games*. There was somber silence disrupted by periodic outbursts of heated arguments as siblings fought over the smallest imaginable offense. In those households, the atmosphere was toxic. It often seemed as if family members endured one another rather than enjoyed each other. I'm grateful I grew up in a home and with an extended family that knew how to enjoy life together.

Our family discovered that having a happy home doesn't depend on income or square footage; it hinges on attitude. Joyful families continually look for opportunities to turn ordinary experiences into happy memories. Here are a few examples from our family:

Most families travel together in a vehicle. Those trips provide great opportunities to make memories. When I (Carrie) was growing up, we lived in a small bedroom community outside the city of Calgary. We frequently drove into the city for appointments or to go shopping. Our family often chose to make the half-hour trip an adventure. My mom would pack a road lunch that we inhaled as soon as we left our driveway. We listened to funny CDs or laughed about something a family member (or one of our marginally insane aunts) had recently done. I was often disappointed when we finally arrived at the destination, since we were having such a good time on the journey.

My family grew up in Canada, so naturally our favorite sport is hockey. Like many families, we watched games together on TV, but my dad instigated our own family fantasy hockey pool. Each year, he and my brothers draft NHL hockey players and then follow them with an Internet hockey pool program. On "draft day," my father hypes the event as though it were a joint session of Congress. As the participants (the group has expanded as my brothers acquired wives) make their draft picks, Dad makes pronouncements so grandiose that you would think the fate of the civilized world hung in the balance. My dad, the king of "sports trash talk," playfully boasts that he'll have the title wrapped up by Christmas and begins looking for the perfect spot in his office to display the coveted trophy (despite the fact that the last time he won, *Leave it to Beaver* was still airing original broadcasts). Whenever someone earns a bunch of points, the others can expect a gloating message within the hour. My sister-in-law, who works for my dad, once called him from the office to gleefully report the newsflash that his top-scoring player had just broken his leg—and she did it on company time!

The year it began, Dad went out and bought the largest trophy he could find. It is labeled "The Blackaby Cup." On it is engraved: "In recognition of superior hockey genius in winning the annual hockey pool." The revered cup has plaques from each year listing the first, second, and third place finishers. It's hideous, so Mom tries to keep it in the garage or laundry room. Somehow, it always finds its way back to the most prominent spot in the house.

Life can be difficult at times. That's why parents owe it to their children to teach them not only how to advance through life, but also to enjoy the adventure. The key is not the methods you use, but the attitude. Odds are good you won't be competing for a Blackaby Cup any time soon, but there may be some fun ideas your family dreams up that generate laughter in your home for years to come.

Enjoying God

There are innumerable ways to make a home a happy place, but of course, Christian parents don't simply want to teach their children how to enjoy life. They also want them to enjoy Christ. There's a reason many people associate Christianity with restrictions and a dull life. It's because many Christians are living restricted and dull lives! Here are a few suggestions for taking the dourness out of your home and replacing it with the joy of the Lord, the Author of life.

1. Emphasize relationship over rules.

If you interview young adults and ask them why they left the faith of their parents, they often refer to the numerous restrictions they endured while growing up. They view their family's religion as negative, condemning, and boring. They recall how their parents refused to allow them to dance, or go to movies, or watch certain programs on television, or listen to "questionable" music. Some complain that they were not allowed to go trick or treating on Halloween or to enjoy other holidays like their friends did. To them, being a Christian was a form of bondage they were eager to be liberated from. These young adults might still claim to believe in God, but they don't intend to practice their faith in the same joyless manner as their parents.

The solution is not for parents to do a 180-degree turn and start condoning activities that go against their values. The problem is when parents focus too much on what their children *cannot* do, rather than inspiring them with the limitless possibilities that are theirs as Christians.

There were some teenagers in my (Carrie) youth group whose parents constantly warned them not to party, drink, or smoke. But as soon as these kids graduated from high school (some didn't even wait that long) they became *obsessed* with alcohol and cigarettes! They looked out from the confines of their restricted existence and saw the pleasures that other worldly kids were enjoying (or pretending to enjoy), and they could hardly wait to join the fun.

Ask yourself this question: Based on the way I act, would my children conclude that Christianity is about rules, or about enjoying a relationship with Jesus? Knowing Christ brings joy (John 15:11). A religion based on rules stifles the spirit. The rules aren't the problem. I (Richard) have never used drugs or smoked a cigarette. Neither did my parents. Neither did my kids. Why? Because those things held no allure for us. We grew up feeling that the secular world was missing out on the fun, not us.

2. Make going to church fun.

There are certain aspects to going to church that are unappealing to most people. The time is one issue. Why can Sunday mornings seem so exhausting, even when you get up later than you normally do on a week day? You also generally get dressed up. Most children don't enjoy doing that. You are supposed to sit still in church, which can be a torturous exercise if you are a five-year-old boy (or an ADD teenager). Going to church has a few strikes against it. So, how do parents make church something their kids look forward to rather than dread?

At times, parents can be so focused on their own needs they neglect their important obligation to help their children enjoy going to church. Dad might wake up on Sunday morning exhausted after a sleepless night. He's grumpy and impatient with the rest of the family. He mutters under his breath when an elderly driver in front of him doddles along and makes him miss a green light. He groans because all the best parking spots are taken by the time he pulls into the church lot. He sits somberly in his pew, never singing or smiling during the worship time. He doesn't open his Bible or follow along during the preacher's sermon. He taps his son when he begins to squirm during the service. He rushes his family home for a hurried lunch so he can be in place in front of the television when the game begins. Years later, this same father shakes his head in bewilderment when his adult son claims he no longer has time, or interest, in attending church.

It is a primary responsibility of parents to make going to church fun for their children. Here are some ways Lisa and I (Richard) did that in our home:

- We tried (not always successfully) to be upbeat and positive as we got our children ready to go to church. Part of this plan involved preparing on Saturday evening by laying out clothes for the next morning.

- We determined never to speak badly about the church, its leaders, or its people in front of the kids.

- We tried to make Sunday lunch a fun experience. At times we'd go out for fast food with other families. Other times we'd make our kids' favorite meals at home.

- We encouraged our children to invite church friends over to spend the afternoon. Sunday afternoons can be great for having a nap, or enjoying peace and quiet. But we were prepared to sacrifice some tranquility if it transformed Sundays into our children's favorite day of the week.

- We avoided conflict as much as possible. For example, if our son dressed in his favorite rock band's T-shirt for church, we had to decide if it was worth mentioning. To us, it wasn't important in the big scheme of things. Or, if someone was running late one morning, we had to determine if chastising him or honking the horn was worth ruining everyone's mood on the way to church.

- When necessary, we did what we could to put a positive spin on a less-than-thrilling experience. Sometimes when the regular pastor wasn't there, we might get a boring speaker. Or one of our children's Sunday School teachers might get into a laboriously dull funk. We'd be prepared to salvage what might have been a hard day for one of our kids. It might look something like this:

Lisa: "Carrie, what did you learn at church this morning?"
Carrie, age 3: "God made birds."
Lisa: "That's wonderful. Daniel, what was your lesson about?"
Daniel, age 7: "Be kind to one another. Matthew 22:39."
Lisa: "Terrific! Mike, how about you?"
Mike, age 9: "We studied eschatological nuances of the rapture in the context of premillennial dispensationalism according to the Book of Revelation."
Lisa: "Oh, I see. Here's a dollar."

Consider what kind of experience your children are having as they go to church each week. Is it enjoyable? Is it drudgery? You may not be able to give your pastor more engaging sermons, or the worship team more upbeat music, but you certainly have numerous options at your disposal to help your family have fun as they attend.

3. Help your children make friends at church.

Children will enjoy church activities better if they have friends. We knew some children at church who would make good companions for our kids, so we steered our children toward them and invited them over to our house after church. The result? Our children looked forward to seeing their friends at church. Even on those occasions when Sunday School was dull or the message was long, they would have had all of their fingernails yanked from their fingers before they would have skipped church. By the way, some parents, for various reasons, require their teenagers to sit with them during Sunday services. We didn't. Our kids and their friends all sat together, taking up several rows. It was a welcome sight to see all those young faces together and knowing they were hearing God's Word.

We also enlisted "cool" young adults from our congregation that we knew our children admired to help us out. Over the years, there were many college students and young married couples who grew to love our kids and who would go out of their way to encourage them. All we had to do was ask.

4. Find another church.

Hopefully, this final option won't be necessary. It is not a decision to take lightly or act upon without prayer and careful consideration. But let's face it. Some churches are a disaster. The adults are constantly bickering. The pastor is boring and uninspired. The children are divided into cliques. As a result, your best option may be to find a church that your children enjoy attending.

Thankfully, our family never had to do that, but we knew some who did. The parents were willing to change churches for the sake of their children, even though they, as adults, enjoyed their former congregation. One such family moved to our church so their son could be involved in our youth group. To this day, that young man is a strong Christian and a close friend of our children. Conventional wisdom argues that you can't swap out your church every time your children become bored, so it's better to teach them to make the best of it. The first part of that statement is absolutely true, and we are *not* talking about hopping from church to church based simply on which one is currently the most fun. But the reality is, sometimes it's the parents who should make the best of a situation, not the children. If your child is withering spiritually, has no friends, and throws a fit every Sunday morning when it's time to go to church, you ought to pray about whether or not there is a different congregation where your child could fit in and find joy.

> *Mom: We don't have to teach our children that life isn't always a party; the world will teach them that. We need to help them learn how to find joy in everyday life and to enjoy the journey.*

All for Onesies and Onesies for All!

The invitation to my brother Mike and me (Carrie) was straight-forward enough. A girl in the college group had moved into a new apartment and was having a housewarming party. We were to arrive at 7:00 with chips or soft drinks or basically anything edible. Oh, and one more thing—we were supposed to wear a onesie.[11] Not owning a suitable onesie in the latest trending color, I had to swing by Wal Mart to pick one up.

Now I should probably interject at this point that I pride myself in my fashion IQ. I would rather be buried up to my neck in a mound of scorpions than leave my apartment wearing shoes that didn't coordinate with my top and accessories. And, in contrast to many people my age, I typically don't make a habit of going out in public dressed in pajamas. Nevertheless, it was a church party, and my brother and I were invited. If our parents instilled one conviction deeply into their children's souls, it was this: When it comes to parties, go big or go home.

So, I found a delightful red onesie that had ridiculous sock monkeys attached to the feet. I had to scrounge through my wardrobe to find matching earrings and a scarf, but I managed. Confession: there was a cute guy in the group who had caught my interest. My brother Mike was on staff as the minister to single adults, and I had been impressed with his friend and right hand man, Sam. I admired the way Sam was such a positive leader among the church's young people (okay, he wasn't too hard on the eyes either). The thought

11 AKA "footie pajamas." For those of you unfamiliar with the cutting edge fashion trend of "onesies," they are one-piece pajamas covering everything from your feet to your neck. They were originally designed for babies to keep them warm when they slept, but they bring out the "baby" in adults, too (especially those with genetically cold feet).

crossed my mind that seeing me wearing a goofy onesie might not attract his attention in the way I hoped, but the party had to go on.

I arrived a few minutes late, curious to see the wide array of zany outfits people were sporting. There was the hostess, wearing a cute camo onesie. There was my brother Mike, game for anything, wearing a black flannel onesie, penguin feet and all. And there was Sam. Oh, my word! This burly, bearded, man's man, was wearing a pale pink onesie with little bunnies plastered all over it! It was the most hilarious and slightly disturbing thing I'd ever seen. I think I suspected at that moment that we were meant for each other. (We got married a few years later.)

But then it dawned on me. We were the only four people at the party who had followed the instructions and showed up in baby pajamas. Everyone else had either been too embarrassed, or insecure, or burdened by a sense of dignity, to be so daring.

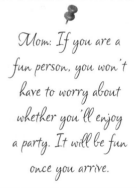

Mom: If you are a fun person, you won't have to worry about whether you'll enjoy a party. It will be fun once you arrive.

The four of us were instant celebrities. Everyone wanted to get a picture taken with us. Word spread throughout the church about how cool we were—well, maybe it was how goofy we looked, but word did spread. One of those photos came back to haunt us in the slideshow at our wedding!

You would have to know me to understand how hard it is for me to appear in public without looking my best. But if you knew how I'd been brought up, you'd also know that I could not look myself in the mirror (and I do that often), if I had not arrived at the onesie party appropriately attired.

My parents taught me that Christianity is a lot of *fun*. I learned that despite all the "hype" the world promotes about its drunken parties and immoral escapades, it is actually *Christians* who know how to have a good time (and we remember the details the next morning). When my church group was hosting an event, no matter how embarrassing, I was going to be there with bells on.

Conclusion

Not every church service is a thrill a minute. Some church events can be downright boring. Rather than wringing your hands and wishing your kids liked Sundays more, or worse, forcing your children to keep doing something they hate, why not initiate necessary changes?

If you have to bully your kids to go to church, you've lost the battle already. Better to do everything within your power to make church enjoyable and attractive. The issue of whether your children grow up loving church or despising it may have less to do with the church and more to do with their parents.

Parents can't legislate their children to love God. But they can stop for ice cream on the way home from church!

One of the most important things parents can do is to model the joy of the Lord, both at church and at home. Jesus said, "These things I have spoken to you, that My joy may remain in you, and your joy may be full." (John. 15:11) The psalmist declared: "In Your presence is fullness of joy." (Psalms. 16:11) The lesson is clear: Christianity ought to be a blast! Is it for your family?

Reflect and Respond

1. Is your home a happy place? What is the evidence?

2. Do others enjoy coming to your house? How often do you have guests over? How often do people indicate they'd like to come over?

3. Is going to church a joyful experience for your children? How could you make it more fun?

4. Are you a joyful person to be around? How often do people hear you laugh? How often do you inspire other people to laugh?

5. Do you tend to pile tasks and expectations onto your children, or do you create fun memories with them?

Action Ideas

1. Make a paper chain to count down the days until an upcoming fun event. (Carrie still does this!)

2. Be proactive this week in preparation for Sunday. Challenge your children to find ways to make Sunday mornings more pleasant. Set out outfits the evening before. Have convenient breakfast food available. Determine to be in a good mood yourself.

3. Don't get stuck in a rut on Sundays, regardless of your traditions! Catch your children by surprise one Sunday after church. Go on a picnic. Make your children's favorite meal.

4. During a stressful week, hide candies or special treats around your house so that your children find them throughout the day.

5. If, because of your convictions, your children will not be participating in something, such as a school dance, then be intentional about replacing it with a fun family outing.

6. Be intentional about inviting families from your church who have children the same ages as yours over to your house for a meal. Create opportunities for your children to make more friends at church.

Chapter Ten

The Life of the Party
Rebelling Against Boring Homes

"Life is either a daring adventure or nothing at all."
—Helen Keller

A Covert Mission of the Most Public Variety

All eyes in Guy's Café were focused on us. No one blinked. Sandwiches lay on the table, half-eaten and ignored. Coffee was left to grow lukewarm. The only sound scratching the air was my (Carrie) shaky contralto voice.

"Row row row your boat…" I warbled, keeping to no particular key. The wooden table on which I stood wobbled slightly, so my footing was as uncertain as my pitch.

My friend Olivia was standing beside me. She joined in with her powerful vibrato. *"Row row row your boat…"*

Then followed a third, undefined voice type, and finally a quasi-soprano.

Our quartet sang the familiar round with all the gusto we could manage, adding interpretive movements as we felt led. We were as melodious as a freight train hurtling through a chicken hatchery.

"…dreeeeeeaam…" In perfect unison we drew out the last note. With a flurry of bows, we hopped down from the tabletops.

A few seconds of silence elapsed. The patrons were clearly spellbound (or fighting a gag reflex). Guy, the café proprietor, solemnly approached us and signed our paper with a flourish. "Congratulations. You may now proceed to the next task." Then the audience erupted into boisterous applause.

We rushed out the door and piled into the minivan where our driver (who happened to be my Uncle Jim) awaited us with a recording that would provide our next clue.

The iconic British brogue of the Beatles played. "*Paperback writer...*" followed by a muffled, crackling noise.

"The bookstore!" Rebecca shouted. "That's the next place, Bentley's Books!"

Without a word, Uncle Jim adjusted his sunglasses, stepped on the gas, and sped us toward our next destination. We whooped and hollered in anticipation.

It was my fourteenth birthday party. We'd gone with a thrilling theme that year, based on a popular reality show, *The Amazing Race*. In the TV version, contestants were given clues that sent them traversing multiple continents to find a series of printed messages assigning them terrifying or death-defying tasks. Our budget was considerably smaller, and we were still kids, so we had to modify the format (it took on more of a "death by humiliation" bent), but my parents did an incredible job. They split our group into two teams and assigned each team a driver and a digital recording on which they'd spliced together snippets of famous songs. From each consecutive five-second clip, we had to guess the location of our next mission. Both squads had the same clues, but in a different order.

When we arrived at each venue, the business owner or an employee handed us an envelope containing instructions for an exercise they wanted us to complete. We lived in a fairly small town, so the local business people knew my family and participated with enthusiasm—sometimes a little too much enthusiasm if you ask me (*ahem*...Guy). The challenges included eating an ice cream cone at record speed at Dairy Queen®, three-legged racing down Main Street, running laps at the local rec center, playing toy instruments outside the town's only bookshop until we received a donation (or until Labor Day, whichever came first), serenading the lunch crowd at a busy café, and balancing an egg on a spoon while running around our church building.

Once our crew successfully completed the final assignment, Uncle Jim rushed us to my house (obeying all posted speed limits, of course). We had to arrive before our opponents and their chauffeur (my dad) in order to win the trophy. Then we had the awards ceremony. My mom is a prize fanatic, so there were coincidentally as many prize categories as there were participants.

It took planning ahead and imagination on my parents' part, but that party was incredible. And, the focus of the party was not on me, the birthday girl, but on our whole group making hilarious memories together.

We were big on birthday parties at my house. Actually, we were big on celebrations of any type. My parents believed that Christians should celebrate life, so we seized any excuse to plan a shindig.

What's a Parent to Do?

In the previous chapter, we discussed how to push back on conventional wisdom that suggests children need to grow up as soon as possible and start being responsible. We pointed out that, while being responsible is a good thing, so is having a childhood. Furthermore, life is not meant to be all work and no play. In this chapter, we'd like

175

to get more specific about ways to infuse joy into your home and family.

Over the years, our family became somewhat famous in our small corner of the world for the parties we threw. Many parents have asked us to share ideas with them about ways to liven up their house and host fun parties. In response to so many requests, we are devoting this chapter to several practical ways you can make your home a delightful place to live.

We've all attended social events that are less fun than a trip to the local sewage treatment plant. The host and hostess are tense. The conversation is stilted. The activities are lame. The evening drags on. Many people confess that hosting gatherings is stressful and difficult. That doesn't have to be the case. We believe that with a little effort and a good attitude, any home can become a festive place.

We may appear to be devoting an inordinate amount of space to the frivolous subject of merrymaking. But besides the obvious reprieve from life's weightier concerns, we believe numerous valuable life lessons result when people gather to celebrate a milestone, or a holiday, or practically any occasion for that matter. Furthermore, there are dozens of benefits to living in a home that values laughter.

The world can be extremely hard on families, especially Christian homes. If your children are trying to maintain godly morals and beliefs in our ethically challenged society, they're bound to endure difficult moments. They desperately need a sanctuary where they can have their souls refreshed and their hearts uplifted. That place ought to be their home. No matter how hard their day might have been at school or work, your children ought to be greeted with joy when they walk through the door of their house.

It's in the Bible

The world had waited for centuries for the Messiah to come. All of creation groaned under its sin, longing for redemption. When Jesus was finally born, humanity still had to wait until He grew into manhood. Then, upon His baptism, Jesus was driven into the wilderness for 40 more days and nights in order to be tempted by Satan. It might have seemed that it was taking forever for the Messiah to inaugurate His long-awaited kingdom. Finally, Jesus stepped into the limelight and commenced His public ministry. Incredibly, perhaps, the first miracle the Messiah performed was to save a party from disaster.

Jesus and His disciples were attending a wedding feast in Cana, which was just down the road from Jesus' hometown of Nazareth. The embarrassed family had miscalculated the number of guests who would be attending (or they underestimated how much their thirsty guests would drink) and had run out of wine. This was an unbearably humiliating moment for the host family. Jesus' mother discreetly pulled her Son aside and whispered into His ear, "They have no wine." (John 2:2) It is significant that the first miracle Jesus performed was to infuse a party with joy and enable people to celebrate a special occasion.

Later, Jesus described the kingdom of God like a wedding feast (Matthew 22:1-14). A king was throwing a huge party for his son and he wanted as many people as possible to attend. Even at the end of the Bible, we read: "and the Spirit and the bride say, 'Come!' And let him who hears say, 'Come!' And let him who thirsts come." (Revelation 22:17)

Isn't it interesting that when the Bible describes the Christian life, it often uses the imagery of a party? Parents who want to develop a home in which their children experience genuine Christianity ought to take heed: families that reflect genuine Christianity are homes that know how to party!

Count on this: the world is fervently pushing its version of happiness on your children. You had better be offering them a Christ-honoring alternative.

Challenge

In the following pages, we'll share specific ways we made our home a venue of joy. We don't claim that every waking moment in our house was filled with singing and bliss, but through the years we picked up some good advice and several practical tips from other families that helped us lighten the humdrum of everyday life. Plus, we came up with a few great ideas on our own that we think are worth sharing.

I (Richard) can't count how many times I've had parents tell me that they're willing to do whatever it takes to make their home a fun place for their children, but they fear they aren't creative enough to generate ideas or adept enough to pull them off. If you feel that way, hopefully this chapter will encourage you. Conversely, if you are someone who can host a gathering with ease, or who finds spreading joy to be second nature, we encourage you to share your gift with others for whom making a home cheerful is more challenging. Parenting is not a competition—rather, we should all borrow and learn insights from others to make our homes a happier place.

Here are three general ways we sought to infuse joy into our home, as well as some specific examples of what we did.[12] We hope they will inspire you, or at least entertain you.

1. Transform the ordinary.

One of the best ways to liven up your family life is to make ordinary events extraordinary.

Let's talk about an obvious one first—television. TV is, of course, one of the biggest time-wasters in America, but it can also be a readily available tool for group enjoyment. Our family's television viewing was pretty limited. We watched the occasional NHL hockey game and Discovery Channel's *Shark Week* (possibly the most addictive thing ever that can't be injected).

However, when the show *American Idol* was at its peak of popularity, I (Carrie) became an enthusiastic fan. My friend, Hannah, was into the show, too. It aired on Wednesday nights right after our youth group meeting at church. One week, I invited her to come over and watch it with me. My dad made us huge ice cream sundaes (his specialty) and we had a great time. The next week, a few more kids from church found out about our *American Idol* plans and asked if they could join in the fun. Over the next several Wednesday evenings, our house became the hot spot for the entire youth group, and we could barely pack everyone into the living room. No one was excluded. Even kids who'd previously been uninterested in the show wanted to join in the party. We stocked up on snacks and even rearranged some of the furniture to accommodate the large crowd.

---

12 You can find an earlier discussion on this topic in The Seasons of God: How the Shifting Patterns of Your Life Reveal His Purposes for You (Colorado Springs: Multnomah Publishers, 2012) by Richard Blackaby.

We discovered that something as simple as watching a TV show can morph into the social event of the week, if you make it fun.

My parents also invested in some recreational equipment, including a Ping Pong table—great for playing riotous "Around the World" games during parties. We built a fire pit in the backyard that became a frequent gathering place for family and friends to roast marshmallows, play guitars, and talk about life.

Our pantry was kept stocked and at the ready with various munchies. (There isn't a more unfortunate combination than a crazy family game night and celery sticks). The correlation between great snacks and the number of happy children in the house cannot be overstated.

Winston and That Other Guy

Ordinary objects around the house can serve as convenient props for family fun. For years, two stone lions sat on our front step like sentinels flanking the front door. We dubbed one of them Winston after the famous "Roaring Lion" himself. We called the other one "The Other Guy," and he remained, for the most part, neglected. Winston had a wardrobe more extensive than Kate Middleton's, and Lisa dressed him impeccably for each season, holiday, or party. Depending on the occasion, he sported a top hat and bow tie, a graduation hat, a bandana, a pink Mohawk, a Santa hat, a fake beard (during No-Shave November), or a peace sign necklace. Winston loved to accessorize, so there was no telling what he might be wearing on any given day. On bright sunny days, he had on his sunglasses; rainy days called for an umbrella.

Residents in our subdivision took walks or drove by our house just to see the stone lion's latest apparel. Delivery and service people regularly commented on how Winston brightened their day. A few even asked us to take their picture with him. People started posting pictures on social media of his ever-cycling wardrobe. One friend who lived more than 1,000 miles away enjoyed the Facebook pictures of Winston so much she compiled a photo album called "The Many Faces of Winston" and mailed it to us. Another friend drove over to our house when she knew we were out of town and surreptitiously dressed Winston in her favorite hockey team's jersey. Then she posted the picture on the Internet, taunting us with the proclamation that Winston was supporting her team (not ours) while we were too far away to do anything about it. People had a lot of fun with Winston. Some felt sorry for The Other Guy and petitioned for equal treatment on his behalf. It all started as a whim, but Lisa transformed an inanimate front porch decoration into an ambassador that brought a smile to hundreds of people.

Home Is Where the Baking Is

When I (Richard) was growing up, our family had the smallest house on the block.[13] But when my mom pulled her homemade cinnamon rolls out of the oven, every child within sniffing distance, including some we'd never met before, found an excuse to stop by. Our humble address was always just one batch of baking away from being the hottest venue in the neighborhood.

---

13 Our house was so small that we used a broken-down Mazda in the driveway as a freezer to store food. This worked well all winter when the temperature remained well below freezing. The only risk was inadvertently being out of town the week spring arrived.

Nothing a Good Fairy Can't Fix

My (Richard) paternal grandmother passed away when I was young, but she left a distinct impression on me. She lived in a tiny old house that would normally hold little attraction for preschoolers like my brothers and me. Nevertheless, we loved to visit Grandma because we came to believe that her house was inhabited by good fairies. When we were well-behaved, Grandma would suddenly glance into the parlor and exclaim, "Did you see that? I could have sworn I saw something in there!" We knew what that meant. The good fairy had stopped by. We frantically raced to the parlor and looked behind couch pillows and books. Sure enough, we would find candies hidden throughout the room. It was magical!

Some of you may be aghast that my grandmother "lied" to us about good fairies. I'm fine with parents who have convictions about telling their children things that aren't entirely true (I didn't use good fairies in our home). But almost 50 years later, I still have fond memories of going to Grandma's house. She turned her modest home into an enchanting place her grandchildren loved to visit. I think Grandma was on to something.

Card Game Olympics

When our family played table games or any game at all, it was never a peaceful pastime. It was an Epic Gold Medal-Deciding Match. Everyone conspired together against Dad. No one really cared who won, as long as it *wasn't* Dad. The family knew that on the rare occasions when Dad did triumph in spite of their collusion, he would be impossible to live with for days.

I (Richard) turned gloating into an art form. I postured. I trash talked. I boasted. I worked the subject of my victory smoothly into every conversation. What else could they do but band together to make sure that never happened (I was almost, but not quite, as intolerable when I lost). In reality, I wasn't teaching the kids to win at all costs, because I rarely won. Instead, I was showing my children how to be "all in" when they played a game, and to measure the success of the game, not by who finished first, but by how much laughter occurred during the contest.

Brown Bag Surprises

When our children were in public school, we lived close enough for them to eat lunch at home most of the time. There was no cafeteria, so band practice or other noon-time events sometimes required them to pack a lunch. Lisa had a lot of fun on those occasions. She loved to slip surprises into their lunch bag. These always brought a smile, and often made them burst out laughing. She might enclose a funny cartoon, or draw a picture on their napkin of something she knew would crack them up. She sometimes did unusual things with their sandwich or included a unique treat. She wrote riddles or composed wacky limericks about them. Their school friends loved to join in on the fun, so Lisa occasionally tucked poems or cartoons in the lunch for them, too. Lisa learned that something as mundane as a bag lunch can be transformed into an opportunity for laughter, if you put some effort into it.

Shall We Gather?

This may seem strange, but my (Carrie) parents' king-size bed became our favorite place to hang out as a family. In the evening, my brothers and I often migrated to their bedroom to talk about whatever was on our mind, laugh about funny things we'd done, or reminisce about past experiences and family lore. Even when my brothers and I were teenagers, we maintained the habit of meeting in my parents' room every night before bed. Often that was the only time of the day we were all home together. These family sessions stretched late into the night, since that's when we felt the most talkative. Many times Dad, knowing he had to get up at 5:30 a.m. the next day, would try to draw the meeting to a close at a reasonable hour. Most of the time we ignored him and carried on the festivities until midnight, all while he was sound asleep.

A few years ago when my brothers and I were all in our twenties, we went home for the holidays and took our significant others. On the first evening, we donned our PJs, lumbered into my parents' room, and plopped on the bed to visit. Pretty soon, even the spouses and boyfriend had climbed on to the very crowded king-sized bed and joined in on the storytelling and laughter.

I (Richard) know some couples that made their bedroom off-limits to the kids because they wanted to maintain boundaries. We're all for

Mom: Everyday routines can be drab and forgettable unless you weave in colorful threads of joy to brighten them up. A variegated life is much more appealing than a monochromatic one.

184

boundaries, but sometimes you just have to go with the flow of what works for your children.

Ordinary days don't have to be mundane. With a little imagination, life can be permeated with pleasant surprises for your family.

A Parent's Best Friend

One of the most brilliant masterstrokes Lisa and I (Richard) ever stumbled upon came when our boys were still toddlers and we went to visit Lisa's older sister Connie. Connie and her husband, Gerry, had two pre-teen daughters and a little son at the time. They showed us to a lovely guest room, and we happily unpacked. However, there was no space to hang our clothes in the closet because it was crammed to overflowing. Connie was a minimalist before minimalism was trendy, so it surprised us to see so many superfluous outfits. In fact, most of the clothing did not reflect her tastes at all. There was a natty fur coat, a hideous blazer, a pair of denim overalls, a lab coat, a bright pink tutu, and even a nun's habit. On further inspection we noticed a clown outfit and a giant Tweety Bird outfit. That discovery revolutionized our parenting.

A costume closet is a parent's best friend and it's so easy to assemble. Get a barrel or box and collect funny clothes and hats along with fake beards, mustaches, eyeglasses, and anything else that might make a cool costume.[14] We learned that you never know when you might be in need of a special outfit.

---

14 I (Richard) admit it bothered me sometimes when I noticed that my kids ventured into my closet for any costume connected to nerds and hobos.

Costumes Are Not Just for Parties

Sometimes our family liked to dress for dinner, but not the way the rich and famous do. Instead, everyone took on the persona of another family member. We would each draw a name and grab a few props to present our version of that person. "Dad" usually lugged a boring, thousand-page biography about an obscure historical figure to the table and then buried his nose in it, coming up for air only to take sips from a giant coffee mug. Whoever portrayed Carrie would don as many brand name garments as possible along with a handheld mirror. And so it went: hockey jerseys, hair gel, fake piercings, idiosyncrasies, pet phrases—the possibilities were endless. The only stipulation was that we were careful not to hurt anyone's feelings or touch on sensitive spots (which of course, everyone has). It was hilarious to see one of the kids pretend to stub their toe and hop around on one foot howling. (A signed disclosure statement prevents us from revealing the identity of the person they were imitating. All we can say is it wasn't Richard or any of the kids).

Costumes Are Not Just for Young People

Other times, we'd make movies. The costumes came out again. One of our favorites featured 94-year-old Great-Grandpa Wells, who was in town for a visit. The theme was pirates (as it almost always was). Grandpa Wells, the villain, was decked out in full seaworthy apparel, complete with eye patch and sword. Unfortunately, Gramps suffered a horrible demise when a giant squid (looking conspicuously like a long vacuum hose) pulled him over the side of the ship to a watery grave (behind the sofa).

2. Have fun with the holidays.

Everyone loves eating, and who doesn't salivate at the thought of a Thanksgiving feast? But the turkey dinner doesn't have to be the whole event, or even the main attraction. Why not take advantage of a family gathering to do more than watch football on television and groan about the tonnage you've just consumed? There are numerous games geared specifically for large groups, and many of them are designed to include everyone from preschoolers to Great Grandma. Some of our favorites include Bunco, Scattergories, Ninety-nine, Mennonite Madness, Farkle, and Catchphrase. When our extended family gathers, we love to team the girls against the guys. There are always small prizes for the winners (or the losers, or all of the participants).

Lisa's family (the Cavanaugh clan) is of Irish descent, so on March 17th, she liked to lay the table out in green. We dressed in green and dyed the potatoes (an Irish staple) green. If dessert wasn't already green, we made it so (pistachio cake, anyone?). Luckily, numerous vegetables are already the right color. If your family is linked to a specific country, you could research one of their national holidays and celebrate your heritage in a similar way. (If you are lucky enough to be French, you can do crepes.)

The first day of summer vacation from school was always a great day at our house (as well as for our children's teachers). One year Lisa threw a beach party. The fact that we lived hundreds of miles from the nearest ocean was a minor detail. Lisa brought in water slides, a wading pool, water guns, Beach Boys music, and popsicles.

Our little town had a parade every Labor Day, and our family wouldn't have dreamed of missing it. To be honest, the parade itself was pretty ordinary (the highlight being a bunch of old men driving by in tiny cars), but we would always transform the parade into a major event. We'd haul folding chairs and thermoses of coffee to Main Street, arriving at least an hour early to socialize, because we knew we'd see loads of people from our church, along with most of our neighbors. Our church decorated a float every year, and our group would make a huge noisy fuss when it passed by our spot (we like to think that's why it usually won a prize).

National holidays, fireworks, a 5K run to benefit charity—whatever the occasion might be, we discovered that if you put in a little effort (and pack a lunch), just about any event can become a happy memory.

As we've already mentioned, our costume closet got a lot of use. Our kids and their cousins all loved costume parties. Over the years, we had some memorable ones! For a hillbilly shindig, our living room was converted into a rustic cabin that would have made Daniel Boone feel right at home.

Another time, we turned our house into a psychedelic hippie pad. Everyone arrived in tie-dyed ensembles and wore long stringy wigs and headbands. We put flowers in our hair and made up songs about world peace. Once we recreated the Old West, complete with Pa Cartwright and his three sons. We filmed a silent movie in grainy black and white using subtitles and piano music in the background. One Halloween, we had a punk rock theme and held a "punkin" carving contest.

But the Hollywood Extravaganza was our most spectacular. I (Carrie) was graduating from high school, and we were moving shortly after that from Canada to South Carolina. Naturally, I wanted to throw a party to beat all parties. "Everyone who was anyone" was invited (from my two-year-old cousin to my septuagenarian grandparents). We rolled out a red carpet from the front porch of our house to the street. As the guests arrived in their gowns and finery, they were treated to valet parking (by my uncles). They glided down the red carpet toward the house while the paparazzi (my brothers' friends) leaped out from behind portable palm trees to take their picture. Inside, there was fake champagne, a chocolate fountain, hors d'oeuvres, and shallow conversation. Then the entertainment began. A mysterious rap star in mirrored shades and a leather jacket showed up and strutted down the red carpet. It took us a while to figure out that mom had enlisted a friend from out of town to crash the party.

We sorted the guests into groups of eight and had them perform various impromptu scenes based on movie titles the director (my dad) handed them. Three grandparents served as the judging panel. My mom presented dollar store trophies that vaguely resembled the Oscars (Daniel was a shoo-in for the "Most Inappropriate" award after his impersonation of Britney Spears). Eighty-five people came to join in the fun.

Great parties can be large or small, but my parents wanted this one to be epic! I was 17 years old and facing the prospect of relocating 2,000 miles away from the only hometown I'd ever known. I'd be leaving my, aunts, uncles, cousins, and long-time friends. My parents went to a lot of effort to pull that party off, and I was extremely grateful—but not surprised. After all, my mom is the one who, when Mike started high school, gave him a magnet for his school locker that said, "You can always re-take a class, but you can never re-live a party."

3. Birthdays can be epic!

Birthday parties don't have to be extravagant, but they have enormous potential to spread joy. One of my (Carrie) favorite birthday traditions was "Story Time with Richard." My dad would assign each of my friends a character. Then, as he told an elaborate story, we had to act out whatever he said. If the dog chased the cat, then the actress playing the dog had to bark and chase after the girl who was portraying the cat. If the cat jumped on the table to escape the dog, the cat would leap on to the back of the person (usually one of my brothers) who had been assigned the role of the table. We would videotape the action and then watch it on TV while we ate birthday cake. We started this tradition when I was eight.

When I turned 16, my parents planned a party but omitted the play-acting because they assumed my friends and I were too old to be birds and inanimate objects anymore. My hyper-dramatic teenage friends were so disappointed that they begged my dad to reprise Story Time with Richard. Dad hastily threw together a play on the spot. It was one of our most memorable performances!

Over the years, we came up with some great ideas for birthday parties. One year we had an *I Love Lucy* party, where the girls all came dressed as Lucy Ricardo. We reenacted two of our favorite scenes: "Vitametavegamin" and the chocolate candy conveyer belt.

Another year, when I had developed a fascination with the Scandinavian nation of Sweden, my parents threw me a "Swedish Party." The fact that we have no known Swedish roots and none of us had actually visited the country didn't stop us. We made everyone dress in blue and yellow (Sweden's patriotic colors), ate Swedish meatballs, and held a competition in which each team had to create a skit incorporating as many famous Swedes as possible (ABBA and the Swedish Chef made numerous appearances).

Daniel was born in March. In Canada, that is still the dead of winter, so his parties often involved winter activities, especially hockey. One year, we booked the local ice-skating rink and had our own hockey game. Another year, we took a group of kids to an NHL hockey game.

Mike's birthday is in June. The year he turned 12, he chose to convoy his friends into town for an epic battle of laser tag. We have fond memories of that day because Mike and his posse took a sound drubbing from a group of giggling eight-year-old girls. The next year we held our own Summer Olympic Games (no eight-year-old girls allowed).

Just the thought of planning a birthday party can trigger an anxiety attack or migraine headache for some parents. Others bemoan the effort and expense involved. The point we're trying to communicate is not that a party has to be spectacular or perfect. We aimed for epic a few times, but our parties were never anywhere near perfect. It's notable to me (Richard) that of all the fun birthday parties Carrie mentioned, her favorite one was the least expensive and the easiest to plan.

Mom: Often the only thing holding a child back from doing something fresh and fun is parental permission.

Whether it's a birthday, Independence Day, or Groundhog Day, families should seize opportunities to celebrate life, have fun, and make special memories.

Challenge

This book is about parenting, so you may wonder why we're devoting so much ink to the subject of goofing off and having fun, as opposed to effective ways to teach children to work hard, make sacrifices, and be responsible. I (Richard) believe that kids actually learn those virtues and many more by throwing parties. Here are a few examples:

1. *Creativity*—Children are naturally imaginative. They love to try new things. Too often, parents are so focused on the budget or the clock or the calendar that they stifle their child's creativity. Coming up with unique ways to throw a party teaches children to put their imagination to good use.

2. *Planning*—There are a few things to consider:

- Throwing a party calls for *logistics*. Include your child when you lay out the time schedule: How long will an activity take? How far away is the venue? How many people will fit in a vehicle, or at one table? Make them do the math!

- Party planning involves a *budget*. Set a limit on the cost and have your children prioritize according to what they can or cannot live without at their birthday party. It can be surprising to hear what really matters to them and what doesn't.

- Party planning takes *resourcefulness*. We once created an enchanted forest in our living room by gathering up every green blanket and towel and every potted plant in the house. We already had a small noise-making machine that included the sound of crickets and flowing water. A few stuffed rabbits and a couple of fake birds and it looked like a scene straight out of Disney's *Snow White.* Our family rarely bought ready-made costumes. Lisa is not a seamstress, so sewing them was out of the question, too. But we frequented the local thrift store, and often we swapped out costumes with friends or cousins.

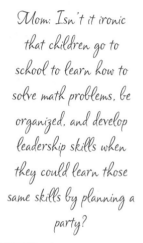

Mom: Isn't it ironic that children go to school to learn how to solve math problems, be organized, and develop leadership skills when they could learn those same skills by planning a party?

3. *Social graces*—According to Daniel Goleman, author of *Emotional Intelligence,* people skills are an invaluable asset in succeeding at work. But many young people are not taught how to be thoughtful of others. Planning a party with your child is one of the best ways to teach and model unselfishness. Probably the most precarious problem connected to hosting social events is when you have to limit the number of invitations you send. As anyone who has ever planned a wedding would agree, this issue is sometimes unavoidable. So, the sooner a child learns how to handle a guest list gracefully, the better.

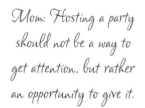

Mom: Hosting a party should not be a way to get attention, but rather an opportunity to give it.

We preferred opening our home to pre-defined groups, like the church youth or the college kids, or the extended family. Having said that, there are times that call for a smaller, more intimate gathering. We didn't always get it right, but we tried to follow two rules of thumb in those instances. First, we sought to include newcomers from our church or neighborhood, those who might appreciate the opportunity to make new friends. Second, we chose to err on the inclusive side—when in doubt, we added another name to the guest list.

Children can learn to be thoughtful as they plan ways to make their guests feel at ease. Whenever we had team events, we always assigned each of our three children to a different group so they could ensure that everyone was included and felt comfortable during the boisterous activities.

4. *Gratitude*—We've heard people say they forego goody bags at their child's party for various reasons, including the cost involved or the effort to assemble them. Some parents say it's enough to feed a houseful of kids and entertain them for a couple of hours, and then send them home with cupcake crumbs on their chin and fond memories.

Lisa was once in a party supply store and overheard a mom veto her little girl's request to have treat bags at her upcoming party. The mom explained to her tearful daughter that it was backwards to give the other kids anything because it wasn't

Mom: The birthday child shouldn't be the only one who receives pleasant surprises at the party.

their birthday. She reasoned that when they had a party, then it would be their time to receive.

Now, no one has elected our family to be the "goody bag police," but we think this custom is a golden opportunity to teach children the art of expressing gratitude. In fact, our family still has a tradition of handing out a small memento to each guest after every party we host. For example, after the hippie party, everyone took home a small, yellow, hippie-themed rubber ducky.[15]

Conclusion

Life may not be a constant party, but it ought to be laced with laughter. We've touched on a few of the countless ways there are to make life memorable and enjoyable for your family.

Likewise, numerous practical benefits come from involving your children in party planning. We mentioned some life skills, but many more could be added to the list (menu planning, cooking, decorating on a budget, and cleaning, to name a few more). Added to those are invaluable social graces, such as being grateful, putting others first, being a good sport, and not taking yourself too seriously.

Mom: Your children will take their cue from you in the way they view everyday life, as well as in the way they celebrate special events.

Having a home that radiates joy doesn't just happen. It results from parents deliberately adding unexpected touches of enchant-

---

15 That party was a few years ago, but people tell us they still have their ducky on display in their home. (Oriental Trading sells party fare like those rubber duckies for cheap.)

ment into the routine of ordinary days. Our goal in sharing our own experience was not to suggest that you copy what we did, but to get you thinking about the countless opportunities around you to spread joy and to make great memories. Be sure to take advantage of them.

Reflect and Respond

1. Is your home a happy place? When was the last time you made a special memory with your family?

2. List the last three social gatherings you hosted in your home. Did you enjoy them? Do you think your guests enjoyed them? How do you know?

3. List the three best parties you ever attended. What made them fun for you?

4. What is something you could do to make your home a more joyful place, not just on the big holidays, but every day?

5. See if you can list 10 skills a child can learn by planning and hosting a party.

Action Ideas

1. Take a few minutes to jot down any fun ideas that you came across in this chapter that you might like to try in your own home. (These can include any memories or ideas that came to you from your own experience.)

2. Make a trip to the Thrift Store (or your own closet) and begin a costume closet. A variety of hats, weird glasses, and gaudy outfits are a must.

3. Set up a game table somewhere in a high traffic area of your house. Put a puzzle or a game on it and invite your kids to join you. Leave the table out for a while to remind everyone to put their work aside now and then and have some fun.

4. Take a look at the calendar and identify the next minor holiday (like St. Patrick's Day). Begin planning to do something fun for it.

5. List each of your family member's birthdays. Begin planning well in advance how you might make it memorable this year.

6. Stop by a store this week and buy a new board game. Hide it away and on the first free occasion your family has, pull it out and play it together.

Chapter Eleven

Of Course My Parents Made My Dioramas

Rebelling Against Hands-Off Parenting

"Be an opener of doors for such as come after thee, and do not try to make the universe a blind alley."
—*Ralph Waldo Emerson*

To Tell the Truth

I (Carrie) was one of those kids who liked school. For the most part, I thought it was fun.[16] But every Achilles has his heel, and mine was science. And so it happened that on a deceptively sunny day in October, my fourth grade classmates and I stood fidgeting in the school gymnasium, each clutching a bulky green trash bag until our name was called. It was Science Project Presentation Day (SPPD). We'd been studying levers and pulleys for months, and we were supposed to create an item that incorporated our accumulated knowledge in some way, and then explain to the class how we made it.

My teacher might as well have asked me to build a working space rocket and land it successfully on Mars. It was no secret in our family that neither Mom nor Dad had a penchant for the sciences. My dad said he got a D in every science class he ever took. It was in my DNA not to understand stuff like DNA. It didn't matter how much I studied; by the second grade, I knew with certainty that I wasn't

---

16 That is, after an epiphany came to me halfway through first grade that the reason I was so clumsy with scissors in art class was because I was left-handed, not "challenged."

going to be a Thomas Edison. Collectively, my family could hardly change a light bulb, let alone invent one.

When I first brought my assignment sheet home to my parents, they tossed it back and forth like a hot potato.

"It's your turn. I made Daniel's diorama." "Yes, but I built Mike's labyrinth."

The argument lasted for days. Neither would yield an inch. They were like Congress edging toward a government shutdown.

As they wasted valuable time, the deadline for presentations loomed. Before we knew it, it was the evening before SPPD. We were left with no other choice—we had to call Uncle Perry. As an experienced mechanic, my uncle can build just about anything he puts his mind to, and that's saying a lot. My parents dropped me off at the Davis house with a flurry of promises: they would help my cousins with spelling homework for an entire year and take them for ice cream one Saturday a month until they graduated from high school.

I helped Uncle Perry construct an apparatus that used a piece of wood, a screw, and an elastic band to send a paper airplane soaring through the air. First, he showed me how to make a jig (a prototype). I was fascinated. Then he sawed while I made him a sandwich. Next came the sanding. I fetched him a coffee. Then the paint job. I made cookies with my Auntie Margy.

When it was finished, he insisted on guiding me through each step of the process (particularly the parts I had missed while watching cartoons with my cousins). Then we tried the maiden flight. Our plane soared all the way across the room—we'd pulled it off!

In the gymnasium, I held my airplane launcher and listened as the teacher asked the children, each in turn, to explain their project. Bobby offered an eloquent description of how he constructed his working water purifying system, and Emma masterfully detailed the process involved in making her portable oven. Finally, it was Natasha's turn. She had freckles and was gangly from her summer growth spurt.

"And what did you bring, dear?" asked Teacher.

"A balloon rocket."

"I see! And how did you make your balloon rocket?"

"Oh, I don't know," Natasha said, doe-eyed. "My parents made it while I was outside playing."

We gasped in unison. Teacher clutched her hankie to her bosom. Someone fainted near the back of the gym. We couldn't believe that Natasha had committed the cardinal sin of all students, the Golden Rule of Elementary School. She'd *admitted,* without even attempting a weak veneer of falsehood, that her parents made her project.

So What's the Problem?

Conventional wisdom claims it is unhealthy for parents to do anything for their children that they can do for themselves. The term "helicopter parent" was coined to describe parents who hover nearby, ready to descend and rescue their children from trouble. The media is filled with horror stories of overprotective parents: one mom called the college dean to make sure her son remembered to wear a raincoat to class. A dad confronted his 25-year-old daughter's boss to object when she was passed over for a promotion.

The theory is that children will not grow up to become responsible, successful adults if their parents don't allow them to work out their problems on their own. But that's a broad statement. How much should parents do for their children, and how much should children do for themselves?

Should you set out your kids' clothes for them to wear each day to school? Should you help your teenagers clean their room, make their bed, choose their friends, approve their dates, buy their first car, do their homework, or pay their speeding ticket? Should you help your children once with a particular problem and then leave it to them after that? Should you arrange play dates for your preschoolers, but let them choose their own peer group when they reach adolescence? Should you watch your children flounder in a school subject without helping them so they learn to solve their own problems? Should you insist that your children work a part-time job while they are in school so they learn how to pay their own bills? Where do parents draw the line?

Lisa and I (Richard) received plenty of (mostly unsolicited) advice on this topic when our children were growing up. By far, the most prevalent counsel was to let our kids assume responsibility for as much as possible, as soon as possible. We were warned that over-involvement would lead to codependency—the Black Plague of modern times. Conversely, if we stepped back out of the way and allowed our children to stumble and fall and get back up on their

Mom: Independence is not all it's cracked up to be.

own, they would ultimately achieve the coveted prize of Western society—independence.

We want to challenge the assumption that the greatest good for your children is their independence. Could it be that in your exuberance to steer your children toward self-sufficiency at the earliest possible age, you are potentially doing them more harm than good? Codependence is unhealthy in relationships, but independence is not necessarily the only alternative. Western culture esteems personal autonomy. However, the Bible promotes interdependence.

It's in the Bible

Abe was an attractive young boy. Everyone liked him. He doted on his sister and generally got along well with his brothers. He also demonstrated ample leadership skills at an early age. Abe's father, a respected leader himself, was a devout follower of God. He loved his son and allowed him lots of space to carve out his own path. Even when Abe made monumental blunders, his father did not rush in to help him, but let him learn from his mistakes.

Abe's father sounds like an enlightened, modern parent. But the truth is, his hands-off parenting style proved disastrous not only in his father-son relationship, but also for the whole nation. Abe (Absalom) was the son of King David, and the outcome of his independence was that he murdered his half-brother and violently divided his father's kingdom.

King David is known for many things. He was a fearless warrior, an inspired songwriter, and a brilliant general. But he was a lousy father for most of his life. In fact, David's blended family was the epitome of dysfunctional. David's sons Absalom and Amnon were half-brothers. Amnon began to lust after his half-sister Tamar, yet David failed to help his amorous son channel his physical passions into an honorable marriage (2 Samuel 13). When Amnon callously raped Tamar, David got angry but did nothing (2 Samuel 13:21), and the strife within his family escalated. Absalom murdered Amnon for defiling his sister and then went into exile, but David still chose not to intervene (2 Samuel 13:36-39).

Eventually Absalom returned to Jerusalem, but David did not reach out to his troubled son for two years (2 Samuel 14:28). The Bible reports that Absalom demonstrated initiative and leadership skills by interacting with disgruntled citizens at the gates of the city each morning (2 Samuel 15:1-9). No one could fault Absalom's work ethic. But the truth was that both Amnon and Absalom desperately needed parental guidance, and Tamar needed protection. Nevertheless, David chose to remain uninvolved.

A well-known Biblical passage explains how parents can use the routines of daily life to teach children about God's ways. As the Israelites waited to enter the Promised Land, God gave parents these directions:

"Teach [God's laws] diligently to your children, and [you] shall talk of them when you sit in your house, when you walk by the way, when you lie down, and when you rise up. You shall bind them as a sign on your hand, and they shall be as frontlets between your eyes. You shall write them on the doorposts of your house and on your gates." (Deuteronomy 6:7-9)

These verses paint a clear picture of the active role God wants parents to take in their children's instruction. The Lord didn't intend for young people to figure out life on their own. He expects parents to interact and engage with their children throughout the day, whether it is while shuttling them to appointments or sitting with them at the dinner table. Everyday life is a classroom in which parents teach the next generation spiritual truths and life skills. Yet, many parents decline to become involved in their children's daily affairs. Instead, they entrust the guidance of their young ones to schoolteachers, youth workers, coaches, and peers. Parents are responsible for the ultimate well-being of their children. How can parents fulfill this obligation if they distance themselves from their children in order to give them "space to grow?"

The pendulum has swung so far in the direction of non-intervention that parents who want to walk closely with their children past the age of 12 years old or, heaven forbid, through their teens and young adulthood, are chastised and ridiculed for being rescuers. The prevailing sentiment is that these over-protected children will grow up to be lazy social misfits who lack initiative. But let's consider the question of parental involvement from a different perspective.

What's a Parent to Do?

An interesting debate arose during World War One. Air Force pilots originally flew their planes without being equipped with a parachute. When parachutes were introduced, some analysts argued against providing them to the pilots, speculating that at the first sign of trouble, they would abandon their aircraft and parachute to the ground. Other experts disagreed, and predicted—correctly— that the added security of this potential means of escape would motivate pilots to fight more bravely.

Parents should be like parachutes. Overbearing and tactless parents can embarrass their children and erode their self-confidence. But removing parental protection can also have disastrous consequences. The older the children get, the less visible the support should be, but it should still be there. Knowing they have backup can make a world of difference in a young person's poise and sense of security.

Caring parents don't want to smother their children, but neither do they want to abandon them in their time of need. The question of how active and visible parents should be in their children's lives is multi-faceted and therefore, trying to give a simplistic answer would be ridiculous. In fact, this one topic is broad enough to warrant an entire book, rather than just a chapter, and, as we've said from the outset, this book is not a missive on what every parent should or should not do. But, it is our desire to probe beneath the surface of assumptions that we consider to be misleading.

Challenge

Below are three instances of conventional wisdom that can actually lead to harmful parenting practices if followed indiscriminately.

I. *Caution*: If parents "bail them out," children won't learn to face the consequences of their actions.

On the other hand: Everyday life affords children numerous opportunities to comprehend that actions have consequences. What they need to learn from their parents is how to show grace to others. They should experience how it feels to be allowed a second chance. Children's mistakes can be valuable opportunities for parents to model forgiveness.

When our boys were young, they loved to set up a hockey net in our driveway and shoot pucks at it. They frequently missed their target. One day, one of Mike's wilder shots broke a window in the garage door. Many parenting gurus would advise that he should pay a price for his carelessness by replacing the window with his own money, or perhaps the hockey gear

Mom: Extending grace to others is more caught than taught.

should be confiscated for a week or two. Then he would learn to be more careful. Or, at the very least, Mike deserved a good tongue-lashing and a heartfelt speech about responsibility.

Lisa and I (Richard) chose to do none of the above. We simply told Mike to turn the hockey net around so it faced the neighbor's house and not ours (okay, that was a joke). But we didn't punish him or even make him pay for a new window. We knew he had not meant any harm. We also were aware that he had no money. Furthermore, we understood that Mike was genuinely remorseful over breaking the window. So we simply got it fixed and encouraged him to be more careful.

We didn't ignore the problem of the broken window and hope it somehow fixed itself (remember the earlier example of King David's parenting?). But Mike now understood that errant projectiles are apt to cause costly damage. He didn't need to sit in his room "thinking about it" for two hours to get the point. He never broke another window (and his aim slowly improved). Now, if Mike had gone on to regularly shatter windows with hockey pucks, we would have certainly stiffened the consequences, but we never had to. He knew broken windows cost money to replace, and he didn't want his parents to have to buy any more. We extended grace to him, and he appreciated a second chance to be more careful.

Am I saying it's patently wrong to have a child atone in some way for costly carelessness? Of course not. I'm just saying that in Mike's case, we felt it was more important to show him grace.

Here's an interesting addendum to Mike's story. Several months later, I (Richard) was taking Mike and his friends into the city for a birthday party outing. In the commotion of a minivan filled with boisterous boys, I failed to notice a pedestrian waiting to cross the street. This was not an intersection with traffic lights, but the crossing was marked by white lines, which meant I should have stopped. Immediately, a policeman pulled me over and gave me a ticket for my misdemeanor. It was somewhat humbling for that to happen in front of Mike and his friends. When we arrived at the venue, Mike discreetly approached me and tried to hand me all of the money he had received for his birthday. He said I would never have gotten the ticket if I hadn't been transporting him and his friends that day so he wanted to contribute what he could toward the cost. It was a very special father/son moment. Of course, I declined his offer.

It occurred to me that Mike had learned more than one important lesson from the garage door incident. Yes, he learned not to launch hard objects toward glass. But he also felt what it was like to receive grace. And now, here he was, offering to help pay for my mistake by sacrificing every dime he had. What could have been a cause for conflict and contention in our driveway earlier that spring turned out to be a learning experience for my son and blessing in disguise for his error-prone dad. I can't count how many times others have commented to me through the years that Mike is a thoughtful, gracious person. I know he gets that mostly from his mother, but I like to remember the small part I played, too!

II. *Caution*: Young people must be allowed to tackle challenges on their own so they achieve a sense of autonomy and empowerment.

On the other hand: The confidence a child gains from "success with assistance" outweighs the humiliation of trying and failing something that is beyond their ability.

Some parents happily dispatch their children to college and conclude their child-rearing days are over. However, Lisa and I (Richard) found that in many ways our most challenging phase of parenting started when our children became young adults.

> *Mom: Parents, not every encounter with your child needs to be a teachable moment. But when they are, make them count!*

If there is one common exhortation I hear over and over, it is that teenagers/young adults must solve their own problems, or they will never be successful in life. Let me tell you a story about Daniel. He was 19 years old, attending college and majoring in English. One of his required classes was taught by a horrific English professor, and I don't use the term horrific lightly. For the sake of prudence, and possibly my own personal safety, I won't tell you her name, but Ms. S was notorious at that school for being hard-nosed. No one is sure what childhood trauma she suffered, or what dark forces lay behind her sinister personality, but on the first day of class, she boasted that two thirds of her students typically never made it to the end of the semester (no one had the courage to ask her if she meant *alive*, or *enrolled*).

When Daniel told me about his class with Ms. S, I urged him to drop the class. I advised him to avoid any professor who prided herself in the attrition rate of her classes. But Daniel explained that hers was a required course. He assured me he would work hard and maintain a good attitude. English was his strong subject, so he was confident that he would be numbered in the surviving "one-third."

Ms. S's lectures were painfully dull, but Daniel forged ahead. He turned in his first term paper, and when he got it back the grade was disappointing, to put it mildly. There were dozens of blood red, disparaging comments in the margins. By this time, it was too late to drop the class without penalty, so Daniel was stuck—and disheartened.

Daniel was at a critical juncture. This was his first year of college, and he had never experienced a professor like Ms. S before. He was bewildered, and his confidence took a major hit. I (Richard) had spent many years in school and had seen just about everything (every university seems to have a Ms. S). I carefully studied the copious red ink smeared across Daniel's paper, looking for clues into his professor's mind. I pointed out to Daniel what it appeared she was looking for, and then helped Daniel devise a plan to ensure his next paper was loaded with it. Daniel's second paper was on a Shakespearian play, Lisa's specialty. We walked through it with Daniel and discussed its themes and issues. We helped him craft his arguments, and then Lisa edited the paper for him.

What a celebration we had when Daniel brought home an A- on his second paper! This time, the red ink was mostly complimentary. Daniel was encouraged. We were relieved. Ms. S was impressed. All was well.

We chose to help Daniel make necessary adjustments so his entire semester was not lost. We taught him how to "read" his professor and to adapt his work to meet her peculiar standards. He ultimately passed that

Mom: Even the Lone Ranger had Tonto.

class, one of only a handful who accomplished that feat. He went on to earn a Bachelor's degree in English, a Master's degree in theology, and is currently finishing a Ph.D. in apologetics. He's also written five books (to date).

Lisa and I have no doubt that we did the right thing for Daniel. We only wonder what would have happened if we had allowed him the "freedom to fail."

III. *Caution:* **Parents and "pampered" children develop a dysfunctional, co-dependent relationship that can result in long-term issues.**

On the other hand: Parents should do what it takes to help their children look and feel their best.

Years ago, one of my (Carrie) favorite Olympic figure skaters gave a dismal performance and botched her chance for a medal. She was deeply disappointed of course, but when a reporter asked her to comment, she simply smiled and said, "Well, I'm still pretty." You may think this sounds like a diva, but quite the contrary, Jennifer

Robinson was known for her humility and winsome personality. My mom and I decided to adopt her mantra, and to this day, when something disappointing happens to me, my mom will console me with the words: "Well, you're still pretty." I often comfort her with the same phrase.

Mom: We teach our children coping skills, not by making them solve their own problems, but by teaching them to seek other's help when necessary.

When I reached puberty, I, like most girls that age, felt like I was anything but pretty. I won't go into detail, but let's just say my feet and teeth grew twice as fast as the rest of me. I wore the same size shoes as my brother, and my smile contained an embarrassing gap between my two front teeth.

Whenever I pointed out one of my flaws to my mom, she would invariably put a positive spin on it. I thought my feet were huge (at size 8), but she told me that Princess Diana and Jacqueline Onassis both wore size 10½ shoes. I worried about my big teeth, but she assured me that when my face "grew into my teeth," I'd have a megawatt smile just like Julia Roberts. And I had a mole on my upper lip that we called my "beauty mark," *a la* Cindy Crawford.

My mom and I went on shopping trips together, and she would help me buy cute clothes. She always knew what was in style. Then we would have a mother/daughter lunch in the food court. I wasn't interested in fashion then, but I loved those outings with just the two of us. We got pedicures. She took me to a dermatologist when I turned 13 to start me on a healthy skin-care regimen. She made sure

I got cool haircuts and encouraged me to highlight my somewhat mousy brown hair. She took me to an orthodontist to get braces. To celebrate when the braces finally came off, we got a teeth-bleaching kit from our dentist to brighten my smile. My mom also educated me in the importance of nutrition and exercise. She drove me to dance lessons, tennis lessons, and, of course, to the arena for figure skating. She went jogging with me. She wanted me to develop lifelong habits that would keep me healthy and fit.

Mom understood the way the female mind works, particularly the middle-school-aged female mind. Some people might think we devoted too much attention (and money) to my appearance. They could argue that superficial beauty isn't as important as good character. People often take the verse "man looks at the outward appearance, but God looks at the heart" (1 Samuel 16:7) to imply that caring about outward beauty is vanity. And when taken too far, it is. But it's also true that we live in a world where the way we look is under constant scrutiny and judgment.

My parents assumed the responsibility of helping me look and act my best. My mother taught me how to apply makeup. She emphasized that makeup is not designed to make you beautiful, but to enhance the beauty God already gave you.

She helped me find trendy but modest clothes and explained that certain types of outfits elicit different responses. I found out later that my parents talked with my brothers about the potentially hurtful effects of teasing young ladies about their appearance. My dad complimented me regularly and noticed if I changed my hairstyle or wore a new outfit, and my mom and dad made a concerted effort to help me feel poised and confident.

One phrase I heard dozens of times from my parents (say, when I was going through orthodontic treatment or buying quality skincare products) was: "You're worth it."

Conventional wisdom said I was being pampered. I'm happy to say that I was! Some could foresee a prima donna in the making, or predict that I would become obsessed with outward appearances. Were my parents training me to be shallow and to value beauty over brains or personality? No, they were teaching me to respect myself, and this was just one of the many ways they encouraged me to be my best.

A child needs self-confidence in order to develop into a successful adult. Unfortunately, the world has numerous ways to tear kids down. I have known several beautiful, talented, and bright girls who suffered from eating disorders and showed other signs of low self-esteem. It makes no sense, but schools are filled with insecure and immature peers who make unkind comments. Especially in the middle school years, kids are made fun of for being too fat or too tall, having a bad complexion, being terrible at sports, getting bad grades, or earning too many good grades. Criticism is widespread and schools abound with bullies. Parents who are willing to invest the time, energy, and finances necessary to help their children be their best are doing them a bigger favor than just giving them a pep talk about how "none of that stuff really matters." Because it does.

Mom: Bullies are a sad reality of our fallen world. Children must be taught how to effectively deal with them.

Oh, Now I Get It!

One day during my (Carrie) senior year of college, while my mom and I ran errands together, our conversation turned to the topic of physical appearance. I asked her why she had always been so concerned about the way I presented myself (down to reminding me to remove my nail polish when it chipped!).

She said she wanted me to know that I deserve to be treated well by others and by myself. She said that the better I cared for my health and my appearance, the more I would respect myself and the better others would treat me. And then she added the customary, "Because you're worth it."

> *Mom: You should teach your children modesty. But don't miss opportunities to help them shine.*

Conclusion

Could it be that children left to solve problems on their own end up feeling powerless rather than empowered? Is teaching your child to "cope" (to survive, to get by, to manage) without the aid of parents really an honorable objective? We don't think so. When you help your children succeed, it communicates that you care and you believe in them. It is our observation that the vast majority of young people wish their parents were more involved, not less.

Everyone needs to know they have someone in their corner. Lisa and I (Richard) did our best to be strong supporters of our children. At major moments in our children's lives, we wanted them to know we were their biggest fans. Of course, there are all kinds of fans; just go to a Little League game and you'll see. Some fans are on their feet the entire game, shouting and waving banners. Others sit quietly and clap discreetly when their child scores a goal. Over the course of rearing our children, we did both. The key for us was never how we cheered on our children, but that we were in the stands.

Mom: Be your children's advocate. Their well-being depends on it.

At times, your children need to see your support and unconditional love for them far more than they need to accomplish another task independently. A criticism of parental involvement is that it makes children less independent. But we would counter that, like the pilots with parachutes, as children face an uncertain future, just knowing they have the full, unwavering support of their family can provide them greater confidence. Who but a parent knows the nerve-racking experience of cheering your child on in a sport, or watching them sing a solo, or play an instrument, or give a speech?

Sometimes, parents do need to back off and allow children more space. But we decided that if we were going to err, it would be on the side of being too involved, rather than not enough. Through it all, our children knew we were on their side, and no matter what they needed, no matter how difficult the problem, no matter what time of night, they could call on us, and we would be there.

Reflect and Respond

1. List three ways you are actively involved in your child's life. (These may relate to school, relationships, sports and so on.)

2. Are you more concerned about your children achieving independence or about helping them succeed?

3. Do you find yourself regularly experiencing conflict with one of your children? Why do you think that is? Do your children know you are on their side?

4. What is a way you recently demonstrated that you are an advocate for your child? Did your child get the message?

5. What are some specific ways you could instill confidence into your children?

Action Ideas

1. Have a heart-to-heart conversation with each of your children, no matter what their age. Ask them how involved they want you to be in their lives. Ask for their feedback about the way you interact with them and if they need more or less space from you.

2. Do an unsolicited favor for each child. Maybe clean their room or do something to help them "keep up" with life. Assure them there are no strings attached. You just care.

3. Identify the major challenges each of your children is currently facing. Prayerfully consider practical ways you can champion their cause without being too intrusive.

4. Surprise your child with an afternoon or evening that is "all about them." They get to choose the food and activity. When they ask why, explain that they are worth it to you.

5. Let each of your children know you pray for them regularly. Even when there is nothing specific you can do to help them, they need to know you regularly pray for them.

Chapter Twelve

Hey, Wait for Me! I'm a Late Bloomer.

Rebelling Against Rushed Childhoods

"Growing old is mandatory; growing up is optional."
—Chili Davis

Parable of the Lost Jeep

I (Carrie) should have known from the beginning that the day would be disastrous. The rain shooting at my bedroom window like bullets, the inky sky, and the rumbling thunder were all good reasons to stay in bed. But that wasn't an option.

I was a 17-year-old newcomer to the South, a land where people are known for their friendliness, but their driving terrified me. I was about to commute 40 minutes on unfamiliar country roads to a new school, all alone, in a foreign land, in the torrential rain. *Cue the melancholic violins…*

Behind the wheel of my trusty, fire-engine-red Jeep, I mustered up the courage to venture out into the storm.

As I turned into the university's commuter parking lot 40 minutes later, my eyes flickered toward the clock: 7:50 a.m. Made it with 10 minutes to spare. I smiled, casually scanning the lot for an open stall. It was completely packed. I guess even the slackers show up the first week. I circled through again. And again.

Then I saw it. Across the street and just down the way was a vacant gravel lot. Granted, it looked like a hub for gang fights and drug deals rather than a piece of real estate intended for student parking. In fact, it called to mind the setting for an episode of *Criminal Minds*. I had a choice—an eerie gravel parking lot, or walking into class late.

Pebbles crunched under my tires as I maneuvered across the ominous terrain. The wind howled like a zombie giving birth.

Three hours later, when I exited the school building, the sky was still a mass of dark clouds and the mid-afternoon light was dim. I pulled my thin hood up, angry with myself for forgetting to bring an umbrella. I lowered my head, clutched my book bag close to my body, and made a dash for it. When I reached the deserted expanse, my stomach tightened.

My Jeep was gone.

A jolt of rage swept through me. I had been *warned* that crime rates in the South were high. Then I realized what I had to do. Quivering, my fingers darted across the keypad of my phone as the rain streamed down my face.

"Hello?" It was the comforting sound of my dad's voice.

An hour later, from inside the warmth of his Chrysler, Dad had me retrace the exact route I'd taken that morning. I railed to his sympathetic ears about the atrocity of auto theft.

As we pulled into the lot, I stopped mid-rant.

There in the center of the lot was my bright red Jeep—*exactly* where I'd left it.

Apparently, in my haste to get out of the typhoon, I'd rushed out of class in the wrong direction and into the wrong creepy gravel lot. (I mean, sheesh. How many creepy gravel parking lots does one small liberal arts college need?)

To my immense relief, Dad only laughed and told me about the time he almost sideswiped a police car the day before his road test.

So What's the Problem?

Being a parent involves a seemingly endless succession of judgment calls. Is my child ready for potty training? Kindergarten? Sleepovers? Dating? Driving? Marriage? As a dad, I (Richard) found myself second-guessing my decisions on more than one occasion—did I push my children too hard, or was I not aggressive enough?

The question is not whether a child will move from one stage of life to the next. That's a given (well, with the exception of Mick Jagger and his band). The real issue hinges on timing. I've heard it said numerous times and in many different ways that the sooner kids grow up and learn how to face life's challenges, the better off they'll be.

Certainly, our culture echoes that message. Kindergarten was once an optional opportunity designed to help a five-year-old child's transition from home to formal education. But now, preschool has been added up front to make sure three and four-year-old kids are ready for kindergarten. At 16 years old, you are deemed capable of driving, and an 18-year-old can vote and join the military. Society has established standards and laws for when you can "responsibly" drink alcohol to when you are old enough to get married. Much of the trouble teenagers find themselves in is because of the barrage of pressure and expectations that assaults them before they are emotionally or physically ready to handle it.

What's a Parent to Do?

Parents can feel enormous pressure to keep up to the pace others are setting for their children. Our family opted not to enroll our children in formal preschool programs. Carrie's birthday fell just short of the cut-off for grade placement, meaning that she started kindergarten at age four instead of five. Many of her classmates were almost a full year older than she was. In fact, throughout her school years, Carrie was almost always the youngest student in her class.

A school classroom is a competitive place where your personal performance is regularly evaluated. You are also constantly being compared to your classmates. We weren't too worried about that in Carrie's case, though, because she was a smart child and eager to go to school like her brothers. She had the general skills required to succeed: she knew her colors and her alphabet, could print her name, and Daniel had taught her how to tie her shoes.

What Lisa and I hadn't foreseen was that Carrie was not yet emotionally or physically ready to begin attending school. She enjoyed classroom activities and made friends, but she struggled with being away from her mom every day, and she loathed the early morning bus rides. She got sick several times that year, coming down with various ailments. She developed separation anxiety. Kindergarten was only half days, so Lisa picked her up every day at noon. But one day, a malfunctioning railroad crossing caused a 15-minute traffic delay (unheard of in our small town). That was back in the pre-cell phone era, so Lisa had no way to let the teacher know. By the time Lisa got to school, Carrie was distraught.

By the end of the school year, however, the adjustment problems seemed to have sorted themselves out.

First grade meant full days at school. Carrie loved her teacher, performed well, and had some sweet friends. But by Christmas break, she had missed more than 20 days of school due to illness. Lisa was beside herself, trying to figure out how she was caring for her daughter so poorly that her daughter could not physically cope with the rigors of first grade.

Several visits to the doctor assured us that she was a healthy child. Yet the cycle continued—she would barely recover from one cold or flu bug, and another one would hit her. During a parent/teacher meeting, Carrie's teacher assured us that Carrie was a well-liked and well-behaved student. But then the teacher made an interesting comment. She said that in her observation, some students were simply not physically ready to keep the pace and fight the germs and viruses that float around schools, and that every year one or two of her students ended up with numerous absences for that reason. With the teacher's understanding and help, we managed to keep Carrie abreast of her grade level, but she carried some of her apprehensions with her through the rest of her elementary school years.

For example, our Canadian province had standardized testing in grade three. On the day of the math test, Carrie's anxiety over her times tables was so severe that the principal gave her special permission to take the test outside of a classroom setting. She scored 99 out of 100 and chided herself for the one she got wrong. She was barely eight years old.

We are not pointing fingers at the system. Carrie's school administrators and her teachers were extremely accommodating and helpful. We could have held Carrie back for one more year before she started school, but we did not want to stand in the way of progress. We had already bucked the trend in our town by not sending her to preschool, so we assumed it would be detrimental to her future if we held her back for another year. She was a smart little girl, and no one suggested we prevent her from advancing to the next grade, so we did what everyone else was doing. She was our third child, after all, and the system had worked for our boys. But if we had it to do over again, we would not have allowed her to advance through school before she was ready.

Prioritize Your Child's Schedule, Not the School's

We learned a valuable lesson that year: don't let society, or a school system, or conventional wisdom determine what's best for your child. We began to look for signs of readiness in our children and did not push them into the next stage of life before they were mature enough to handle it. We were able to make more informed decisions in the ensuing years, because we realized what a large role readiness plays in a child's well-being.

It's in the Bible

Notice what Ecclesiastes 3:1 says about growing up: "To everything there is a season, a time for every purpose under heaven." Like nature's seasons, God created us to follow a pattern of growth and maturity.[17] Agriculturalists know that the key to success is not just effort—it's also a matter of timing. You can be as optimistic as you want, but you're wasting your time casting seed on the ground in the dead of winter. Likewise, there is no point trying to harvest a crop before it is ripe. Those

Mom: Transitional periods in your child's life call for your "A game" as a parent.

---

17 A more in depth look at this concept is found in The Seasons of God: How the Shifting Patterns of Your Life Reveal His Purposes for You (Colorado Springs: Multnomah, 2012) by Richard Blackaby.

who work closely with nature know this simple but irrevocable truth: it doesn't matter how eager you are to plant or to bring in the harvest; if it's not the right season, you're going to have to wait.

Challenge

There are unique benefits to each phase of life. Yet parents can be guilty of hurrying their children from one stage to the next without allowing them time to embrace and enjoy the one they are in. Consider the following list and think about the way each of these factors influences our children to grow up too fast:

- Middle school dances

- TV shows, sitcoms, and reality shows

- Movies

- Advanced Placement tests[18]

- Internet

- Social media

- Divorcing parents

- Having a part-time job

- Fashion (TV ads and seductive posters in malls)

- Professional sports, scouting, and scholarships

---

18 These are tests taken in high school that allow students to bypass certain introductory classes in college.

- Drug or alcohol addiction in the family

- Serious illness or death in the family

Ironically, while technology and modern medicine are prolonging the human lifespan well past "three score and ten," we are simultaneously rushing our children through each stage of life and on to the next, as though we're worried they might miss something if they linger in their youth. Four-year-olds have to be "prepped" for kindergarten. Pre-teens attend dances and co-ed parties. Adolescents are sent off to summer sports camps to hone their skills so they can make the team in the fall. Teenagers stress over SAT tests and college entrance exams. College students are afraid to change their major, because it may mean five years of college instead of four. Young adults obsess about finding a spouse, because it seems all their friends are already paired off. We're living in a society where even athletes, once the embodiment of good health and determination, are resorting to performance-enhancing drugs, not just in an effort to win, but so they won't be left behind by other doping competitors.

Mom: Parents have to protect their child's childhood or the world will snatch it away from them.

What's the hurry?

Parents take great delight in watching their babies develop. Grown adults never dreamed they would shout and cheer when another human being achieved control over a bodily function. But here they are, jumping up and down like freshmen at a football game as their son proudly accomplishes his feat. Or parents yell and wildly clap their hands because their yearling just took two awkward steps before collapsing to the floor. School gymnasiums fill up with beaming moms and dads as middle school kids squawk out vaguely discernible tunes on flutes and clarinets.

Life is not a mad dash to the finish line; it's a journey. It's not intended to be guzzled down, but to be enthusiastically savored.

Let's give some thought to a few areas where children are sometimes pushed into a new stage of life before they are ready.

1. Relationships

In times past, elementary school students would have a secret (or not so secret) "crush" on another kid. Today, it's not unusual for thirteen-year-olds to claim they are "in a relationship." In fact, it's often the parents and grandparents who are teasing young people and putting pressure on them to find romance. "Do you have a girlfriend yet, son?" "Sweetheart, is anyone taking you to the dance?"

Even churches contribute to the pressure on their teens. I (Richard) talked with a youth pastor who expressed concern over how fixated the teenagers in his youth group were on members of the opposite sex. As we talked, he casually mentioned that their youth program was sponsoring their annual dance at the church gym that Friday night. I asked the minister what kind of pressure he thought the church dance put on the 14-year-olds in his program to have a boyfriend or girlfriend. The church ought to be a safe place where people are not pressured to conform to unwholesome values. Surely Christian young people ought to be able to attend a church-sponsored event without feeling like a failure if they don't have a date. Relationships with the opposite sex ought not to be rushed into!

2. Jobs

Life for an adult is a balancing act—navigating a career, rearing children, paying bills, caring for aging parents, and addressing physical challenges. Work can be rewarding, but it can also be extremely trying. Everyone learns soon enough that daily existence is not all fun and games. In fact, that is all the more reason to allow our children to enjoy every pleasurable moment they can while they are young. We all know a completely carefree life doesn't even happen in Disney movies (what with mean stepsisters and all), but a kid with a relatively worry-free childhood may possess a stronger foundation for handling life's inevitable difficulties than a youth already beset with burdens and responsibilities.

More than likely, our children will spend many years going to work, but their childhood will soon pass. Parents need to think carefully if it is more important to rush their child into the workforce, or to allow them to gain the full benefit of a rich, creative, pleasurable childhood.

In days gone by, particularly during the Great Depression, scores of children had to quit school and take on jobs to help the family survive. We like to romanticize that era with platitudes about young people learning responsibility and so on. But we overlook the sad reality that a generation of sons and daughters never got to experience a real childhood. Thankfully, there are more enjoyable ways to teach youth a strong work ethic than carting them off to a Charles Dickens-like workhouse.

Lisa and I picked up several ideas from some of the families in our church who were a few years ahead of us in the parenting journey. When school was out for the summer, these parents had their teens go on a youth mission trip, or the family would go on a mission trip together. Many of the teenagers in our church taught Vacation Bible School. Some parents sent their older teenagers to be summer missionaries for a month. This left their child free to go with the family on vacation or to attend youth camp, or simply to spend time with their friends and rest up for the next school year. At our current church, middle school children, as well as teenagers, adopt widows in the congregation and then drop by during their free time each week to mow their lawns and do errands or minor odd jobs in their home. We've watched these teens acquire numerous practical skills that will be helpful to them in the future while absorbing strong Christian values at the same time. Besides working hard, they experienced the intrinsic gratification of serving others without the expectation of a paycheck.

Mom: Don't sweat over "missed opportunities." Instead, focus on getting yourself ready for what is coming.

We are fortunate in North America that our young people have so many opportunities to travel and learn in ways that are broader than just flipping burgers or mixing lattes. Now, we are not knocking burger-flipping or latte-mixing as options, and in fact, our family did those things, too. But before you write off the other possibilities as too expensive or impractical, check with your church or extended family and explore some of the countless creative ways your children can learn by serving and volunteering.

3. College/Career

The question of appropriate timing weighs heavily in the decision of what your son or daughter should do after high school graduation. A college education is expensive due to tuition, the cost of dorm residence or a vehicle for commuting, buying textbooks, and so on. The question of whether a child should take a gap year, enroll in university or a junior college, or attend a trade school is complex, and if we had an answer that suited everyone, we'd be in the consulting business and would be fabulously wealthy.

As I've (Richard) already shared, we learned well before the college years that when it comes to education, one size does not fit all. At various times, we had our children in public school, private school, and homeschool. Over a five-year period, our town was singled out as the most rapidly growing community in the nation, so the schools had to be re-allocated to accommodate the burgeoning enrollment. That meant we had each of our children in a different school, and all three schools were in separate parts of town: Carrie was in elementary school, Daniel was in middle school, and Mike started high school. That year taught us a few things. First, minivans can only put on so many miles before they give up the ghost. Second, when one school bus (and its saintly driver) has to deliver children to three different schools, the alarm clock has to be set for very early in the morning. Third, school pageants, parent-teacher interviews, and concerts can take up an entire week in the month of December.

The diversity of options we pursued when the kids were younger prepared us well for when each of them had to decide what to do after they finished high school. Once again, each of our children chose a different path regarding post-secondary education.

Mike spent a year in a program designed for young adults who desire to strengthen their Bible knowledge and deepen their faith before pursuing a career in whatever field God guides them. That year was pivotal for Mike in many ways, both personally and academically, and it set him on his path to full-time Christian ministry. He was able to transfer his classes to a Christian college for his B.A., and then moved to North Carolina to earn his Master's of Divinity. He then earned a Ph.D. in Christian Apologetics. Today he is a church planter in Victoria, Canada. This is the kid who told me when he was in his senior year in high school, "Dad, I'm not smart enough to go to college."

Daniel chose to take a gap year and travel to several countries doing a wide variety of volunteer work, which included working in remote villages along the Amazon River, ministering to teens in an affluent city in Norway, and serving refugees in Greece. When he returned, he was ready for university. He attended a junior college for two years and then transferred to North Greenville University to complete his Bachelor's degree. He got married the summer after college graduation and moved with his sweet wife across the country to San Francisco to work on a master's degree. Like Mike, he also earned a Ph.D., but his focus is on Christianity and the Arts. He is also living his dream of being an author. He is the first member of the Blackaby family to have books published in both fiction and nonfiction (he is also the first Blackaby author in five generations to write about someone being eaten by a monster).

I (Carrie) finally got over my test anxiety, and my mom no longer had to pry me off of her pant leg to attend school. I have outgrown her nickname for me (which used to be "Velcro"). I entered a bachelor's program the fall following my high school graduation. I've since earned two master's degrees. I can speak for my brothers as well as myself and say we are grateful that our parents were willing to explore educational options that uniquely suited us and that matched our personalities, used our abilities, and set us on the path to fulfill our dreams.

Conclusion

Children are best prepared for adulthood by fully experiencing (and enjoying) the progressive stages of growing up: preschool, childhood, adolescence, and young adulthood. It's up to moms and dads to help their children make important life decisions in a timely way. When children are thrust into situations before they are physically, emotionally, or spiritually ready, the consequences can be painful and long lasting.

Parents have a unique vantage point to determine when a child is ready to take the next step, as well as what their capacity is to handle the requirements of school, relationships, a job, and ultimately, marriage.

That's also why it's so important to thoroughly know your children. You don't want to hold them back when they are ready to take flight, but neither should you boot them out of the nest if they are going to face-plant at the bottom of the tree.

The secret to successful parenting, and thriving in life, is exactly what the Bible says it is: paying close attention to timing and readiness.

One of the best pieces of advice Lisa and I (Richard) ever received was this: explore your options!

When Lisa and I took our first child home from the hospital, our minds were filled with all manner of theories and ideas about how we would rear our children. Many of those grand ideas hit the garbage bin while our kids were still preschoolers. Experience taught us to customize our approach to each child in light of unique personalities and circumstances. It meant we had to do a lot of praying and asking for advice. As it turned out, parenting wasn't what we had expected. It was better.

Mom: No one knows your child better than you. Don't let popular opinion sway you from your own instincts.

Reflect and Respond

1. Does the term *immaturity* have negative connotations for you, such as childish, weak character, imperfection or underperformance, or do you see it as simply a lack of readiness?

2. What are some ways you have adapted your parenting style based on your child's personality and maturity level?

3. Do you recall a time when your child was held back when they were mature enough to move forward? If so, what happened?

4. Are you aware of outside forces influencing your child to grow up too fast? If so, how might you keep that from happening?

Action Ideas

1. Think of an enjoyable activity your children used to do when they were younger. Tell them you are pulling out one of the "golden oldies" and spend the evening doing that activity.

2. Plan ahead for children's summer. What are your goals for them? Do you want them to be able to go to church camp? A mission trip? Do you want them to rest? Do you want them to earn money? Sit down with each child and make a plan so he or she is intentional about making the most of their summer.

3. Consider ways you can help your children mature in a healthy sense. Could you take them on a visit to the hospital or nursing home with you? Could they volunteer to do yard work for a widow? Could they do volunteer work at your church? Make a plan to help your children mature in a healthy, age appropriate, God-honoring manner.

4. Do you sense one of your children is trying to grow up too fast? Intervene and try to find out why. Are the friends he keeps pressuring him? Is she spending too much time on social media? Be diligent to find out why your child wants to grow up so fast.

5. Organize an enjoyable family night. As part of the festivities, take time to reminisce about humorous stories from the past. Help your children remember the fun times they have had as children. Help them learn to embrace and celebrate each stage of their life as it comes.

Chapter Thirteen
"But Dad, I Don't Want to Be an Engineer!"
Rebelling Against Parental Pressure

"Nothing great has ever been accomplished without passion."
—*Georg Wilhelm Friedrick Hegel*

What Should I Be? There Are so Many Sides to Me...

I (Carrie) have loved writing for as long as I can remember. Growing up, my home was crammed full of enough books to rival the Library of Congress. So even before I was old enough to read, I developed a deep appreciation for literature. When I was three years old, I began composing short stories. That I was illiterate was no small obstacle to overcome. But a solution was found: my patient mother would act as my amanuenses. She would transcribe the images in my head onto the page for the masses to love and devour.

Night after night, she crammed herself into my miniature red bed. Coffee in one hand and a pencil in the other, my mom diligently recorded what flowed from my fertile mind through my lips.

The tales varied, but they always involved a three or four-year-old princess who had curly blond hair, two villainous older brothers, and a rag doll named Pilly. Coincidentally, I too had curly blond hair, two villainous older brothers, and a rag doll named Pilly. The narratives often included the Death Star and vicious attacks by aliens from neighboring galaxies. Though my mother was the only person besides myself to ever see these stories, I knew I was impacting the literary world for the better and was well on my way to becoming the next Jane Austen.

Throughout the remainder of my childhood, I flirted with the idea of being a ballerina, a Power Ranger, or a former nun who becomes a governess to seven musical children, marries their dad, and flees the "Nachos," as I called them. But these were all passing fancies. I continued to write and read. By the time I reached high school graduation, it was evident what I should choose as my college major: English (and not just because I needed a calculator to count past single digits, or because my idea of a scientific experiment was trying out a new cookie recipe).

The problem was figuring out what I would do with my English degree once I had it in hand. As far as I knew (and according to many leading experts at *The New York Times*, as well as friends and family who candidly offered me unsolicited advice), there are three career paths for an English major: (1) teach high school; (2) become a Starbucks barista and scribble lines of poetry onto napkins during lunch breaks; (3) marry rich.

None of those options appealed to me (besides the third). But, my parents encouraged me to follow my passion. And I felt God was leading me toward English, so I forged ahead.

I loved studying English. My classes were fascinating and my writing ability improved. My college years flew by and once again I found myself at a crossroads. I knew I wanted to earn a master's degree. But what should I study? One of my professors and mentors encouraged me to pursue a Master of Fine Arts in creative writing.

I applied and was accepted. But the closer I came to the start of the semester, the more I panicked. What was I thinking? What could

I do with a fine arts degree? I envisioned my future vividly: Me. Alone. On a street corner. Bundled in rags and holding a rusty tin can. I'd spend my nights sleeping in back alleys and my days begging for spare change while correcting typos in discarded newspapers.

I frantically researched education programs online. Though I felt no inkling to be an educator, teaching appeared to be a more practical profession—teachers get paid, and schools *always* need teachers! I asked my mom if she could envision me as a teacher. I could tell she was chewing the inside of her cheek to keep from laughing, but she simply reminded me that the teaching profession calls for a measure of patience, and that perhaps I was not "wired that way." *Drat!* I was stuck enrolled in an expensive program that held absolutely no promise for the future.

When my doubts were at their worst, I did what I often do in dire situations—I called an official father/daughter meeting. I told my dad about my concerns. I cried and explained that I was ruining any chance of a happy and meaningful life. He listened patiently, and then instead of telling me what to do, he suggested we take a look at my life history (he's always liked history):

Mom: Parents should nurture their children's passions, not superimpose their own.

- I had loved writing since I was a little kid.

- I graduated *summa cum laude* from university with an English degree and had won the award as the top English student in my graduating class.

- My professor, who was also the head of the English department, told me I was a naturally gifted writer and owed it to myself to develop my skills.

- I clearly had a zeal for writing that I didn't have in the slightest for other pursuits, like nursing (you read about my capacity for compassion when I mentioned my dad's unfortunate inline skating incident), law school, or nuclear physics.

In the end, I commenced with the MFA. I didn't want to look back thirty years later and kick myself for not pursuing my passion when I had the chance.

So What's the Problem?

We saved the prickliest subject for last. It concerns launching your children into the big scary world of adulthood. Two defining decisions generally occur at a time when people are still young enough to dream about being a rock star, and before they have figured out life's mysteries (such as how you can put two socks in a clothes dryer and retrieve only one at the end of the cycle).

The biggest decisions young adults must make in a relatively short period of time are these: 1) Choosing a career and plotting a strategy to become educated/trained for the aforesaid career; 2) Choosing a life partner.

Let's look at these crucial decisions and how parents can help their children make them wisely. We'll start with a story from the Old Testament.

It's in the Bible

Elisha was not an ordinary young man. He was as strong as an ox. Stronger, in fact. He could single-handedly manage twelve yoke of oxen! He was a hard worker and a born leader. He was the perfect choice to take over the farm once his father grew too old. Then, as now, the family business was often entrusted to a family member from the next generation.

One day, the revered prophet Elijah passed by. He tossed his mantle onto the farm boy and invited him to leave his career and join him in the school of the prophets (1 Kings 19:19-21). Elisha didn't even take time to sleep on it! He kissed his parents goodbye, grilled up a pair of oxen, and off he went.

The Bible doesn't describe the father's reaction to seeing his son abandon the family farm, or killing two of his oxen (though, we can guess). But the Scriptures tell us that Elisha became a great prophet and performed many more miracles than had his mentor, Elijah. Clearly, God had a different path in mind for Elisha than what his parents expected.

What's a Parent to Do?

As you know by now, we don't believe parents should ever entirely cut themselves off from assisting their children. As teenagers leave high school, they will make decisions that determine who they build a family with, where they spend the next five decades working, and if they will continue to follow God or abandon their Christian faith.

That is not the time for parents to get careless or to relinquish their parenting duties. Let's take a look at these two monumental milestones.

I. Choosing a career

Conventional wisdom is somewhat divided on this one. There are experts who suggest that at 18 years old, our children are adults and must make their own decisions free from parental interference. These pundits argue that parents must keep their hands off the process, even if it means their children make several false starts into various jobs and careers. This often leads to young adults changing their majors in college several times, or switching jobs repeatedly while trying to find the right fit. American history boasts the likes of John Jacob Astor, John Rockefeller, and Henry Ford, who, through trial and error, managed to find the path to enormous success.

A second common view approaches this watershed moment in peoples' lives as too crucial to entrust solely to the discretion of an 18 year old (when tens of thousands of dollars in tuition may be at stake). Our son's or daughter's future education and career hinges on wise decisions. The problem is that the child has no experience in making important decisions of the magnitude of say, paying tuition, finding health insurance, or buying a car. It seems obvious that our infants-in-grown-up-bodies need parental intervention at this pivotal juncture. For goodness' sake, what does a teenager know about long-term planning, interest rates, or market projections?

Of course, the reason attitudes become conventional wisdom is because they often contain a kernel of truth. As we write this, a glut of freshly graduated law students who incurred massive debt in student loans are discovering that law firms have far fewer openings than law schools have graduates. So, as parents watch the news and hear the prognostications of where future jobs will be found, they try to strategize with their sons and daughters about where they are more likely to find gainful employment. It seems like a responsible and loving thing for parents to do. And it is. But if parents are going to help steer their children into prosperous careers, they would do well to understand that their priorities may not be the same as their children's.

II. Choosing a life partner

Many young people are making poor choices with their marriage partner and are suffering the painful consequences. We believe this area is one in which conventional wisdom has steered parents horribly wrong. One of the most enormous decisions in any person's life is whom to marry. Second to that is when to marry. Yet amazingly, many parents do little to help their child in their choice of spouse or in the timing of their wedding.

Mom: Moments when you feel pressured, worried, or afraid are not the best times to make major decisions.

Some parents blithely assume they have no business helping their children find a spouse. Many simply hope for the best and wait to see whom their child brings home. I (Richard) have heard it said that once people become adults, they should make their own decisions based on the (hopefully strong) foundation their parents laid for them when they were growing up. In part this is true. Lisa and I spent more than twenty years helping our children develop into the kind of people who would make wise decisions. Nonetheless, we certainly were not going to sit back and run the risk that they would marry someone who would break their heart and cast a cloud over their future. There was simply too much at stake.

Mom: Parents, don't bail out before your child's "big" decisions have been made.

Parents must walk the fine line between telling their children what major they should choose in college or what career track they should take, and helping them discover those paths for themselves. The same is true about parental involvement as young people choose a life partner.

Here are a few important factors to consider in the process. Since the decisions at hand involve both parties, we'll direct the first few to the parents and then speak to young adults.

Challenge

To the parents:

1. Consider your personal motives. We tend to want our children to make the most money possible and to live down the street from us so we have easy access to our grandchildren. Our advice is often colored by our own desires. Our child suggests studying to become a nurse; we suggest they enter medical school to become a doctor (since doctors make more money). Our child ponders becoming a chef; we steer them into business school (because they can earn more money). Our child suggests earning a degree in Bible; we pressure them to enter the school of engineering (because that is what we did). We push a certain young lady or young man on our child because we know the family and we like the parents. While our own experience will certainly inform the counsel we give to our children, we need to be sure our advice is focused on our kids and not on us.

2. Encourage your child to take time to enjoy their youth, to learn, and to explore. Many cultures are so squeamish about "wasting" time that they incorrectly label numerous pursuits (such as traveling, staying single, or mission work) as unproductive. They push graduates to take the first job that comes along, or marry the first person who asks them. Twenty years later, those who let themselves be rushed through life have a mid-life crisis because they don't like their job, their spouse, or their life.

Youth is the time to earn as much education, training, and job skills as possible. I (Richard) have spent two decades counseling ministry students, and the most disturbing pattern I see is when some insist on aborting their education because they are tired of school or because they want to start working right away. I always advise them to stay in school to finish their training and trust that, when they are ready, God will guide them to the next step in their career. Unfortunately, I have often sat with people who rushed into a job unprepared. I tried to help them understand that the reason they crashed and burned was *not* because they are a failure as a person, but because they were not ready to take on a position that was beyond their training.

I have had the same type of conversation with those who married the wrong person, or got married too young. We know many people in their early twenties who are already divorced. That typically reflects either stubborn young people who refused to heed any advice as they rushed into a questionable relationship, or parents who did not help their child wisely navigate one of the most important decisions they would ever make.

Modern society urges teenagers to race through life while gobbling up all of its pleasures. But wise parents will help their children understand that youth is the best time to explore. It's a great time to travel, learn about new cultures, and attempt new experiences. Before settling down into a career, or marriage, it is immensely important for them to discover who they are, and it is better to do it as a young adult than as a middle-aged person in crisis.

3. Trust your child. While you don't want to go AWOL on your children at this crucial period of their life, there comes a time when the hands-on phase of your parenting is over. The reality is, if you haven't taught your child by his or her early twenties to have high standards in Christian character, integrity, and purity, your current role will probably be more of a listener than a teacher. That doesn't mean you can't be helpful in many ways, but the time to instill values in your children begins well before they become adults. However, if you have taught your children well, don't continually fret and worry as they progress through life.

> *Mom: Seeking what's best for your child is not the same as getting your way.*

4. Keep the pressure off. I (Carrie) am dismayed when I see parents that are in a hurry to get their child "married off." Moms who think they are just being helpful sometimes end up not only embarrassing their daughter, but also steadily eroding her self-confidence by implying to her and to others that she is desperate. My brothers and I understood that our parents had wisdom to share, and we welcomed their input, to a point. Still, there were times when we gently had to say, "Mom, you may think that person and I would make a charming couple, but I find nocturnal reptiles to be more attractive." There is a bit of a matchmaker in all of us, I guess.

To the kids:

Well-intentioned but outlandish suggestions notwithstanding, I (Carrie) found that my parents had a lot of helpful advice as I inched closer to the life-changing decisions of where to go to school and what to look for in a spouse. Below I'll summarize the essence of what they said to my brothers and me over the years:

1. Seek God's will. God made you and He loves you. He wired you with unique passions and gifts, so He knows better than anyone how you can best spend your life. Walk closely enough with God that you recognize when He is steering you in a particular direction. Pray fervently for wisdom and discernment, and God will give it (Isaiah 30:21).

2. Don't panic. Forget about what Hollywood says. Some things really are worse than being single all of your life—like being married to the wrong person. Keep waiting until the right person comes along, or until God grants you peace and contentment with remaining single. But don't panic and marry someone just so you are married (Proverbs 12:4).

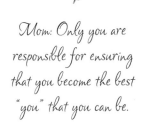

Mom: Only you are responsible for ensuring that you become the best "you" that you can be.

3. Keep working on you. Make the most of your time, set goals and work toward them, and develop healthy, godly disciplines. Don't constantly compare yourselves to others. Take care of yourself physically. Let God grow your character. Become the best person you can be, because *you are worth it* (1 Timothy 4:7-8).

4. Don't cave in or settle for less than God's best for you. Don't be afraid to go against the flow if what others are doing is not right for you. Don't blindly accept what you read, see, or hear at surface value. Check into it. Don't lose hope and lower your standards! Respect yourself enough to hold out as long as you have to until you find God's best.

Conclusion

For life to have meaning, it should consist of more than merely paying off a mortgage and building a retirement fund. These life goals might have been acceptable for previous generations, but they will not satisfy the younger generations. Young adults are trying to find jobs and careers that not only will earn them a comfortable living, but will also satisfy their passions and values. For that, they may need help from their parents.

Some of the most crucial parenting occurs as our children become young adults and choose a life partner. However, while you can't tag along on dates with your child or accompany them on job interviews, you still have a key role to play. You may not be a *caregiver* any more, but you can still fill the critical role of

Mom: The role of a parent never truly ends; it just changes.

consultant. Hopefully, you have developed such a loving and encouraging relationship with your children that, when they face an important decision, you are one of the first people they call.

Reflect and Respond

1. How are you presently preparing your children to make wise career decisions in the future?

2. Do your children have high standards concerning their future marriage partner? What are their standards? Can they articulate them?

3. Are you putting undue pressure on your children about their education or career? Would you be okay if your child took a job that paid less than he or she was capable of earning, but was fulfilling?

4. How involved do you intend to be as your children date and look for a spouse? Are you pushing your young adult son or daughter to get married?

5. Have you developed the kind of relationship with your children so they want you to be involved in making crucial life decisions? If not, what might you do to improve your relationship?

Action Ideas

1. Have your teenager take some aptitude tests (such as Myers-Briggs). Then discuss the results with them. These tests

are not determinative, but they can reflect the skills, passions, and strengths of your children at the time. Talk with them about possible careers in which they could use those skills and interests.

2. When you know the kind of professions your child might be interested in pursuing, seek out people in your church or among your friends with those backgrounds. Have them set up an opportunity for them to talk with your child about what it is like to work in that profession.

3. If a child shows an interest or aptitude for certain jobs, help find opportunities that will provide experience, whether as a volunteer or in a part-time job.

4. If you know a profession your teenager is interested in, keep your eyes open for articles, books, lectures, films, or job fairs that can help your child learn more about that field.

5. If you are a dad, take your teenage daughter on a date. Treat her like a lady. Talk with her about what she should expect from someone who takes her on a date. Encourage her not to compromise her standards for any reason. Help your daughter feel special. Encourage her to expect to be treated well by others who date her as well. If you are a mom, take your son on a date. Explain to him what girls want from a date and how they ought to be treated. Make it fun. Let him know you trust him to be a gentleman when his date isn't his mother!

Epilogue

There once was a father who was brokenhearted about his son. The child struggled with issues that appeared impossible to overcome. Some believed he suffered from an untreatable medical condition. Others suggested there were darker, spiritual causes for the boy's destructive conduct. The only consensus people could reach concerning the boy was that his situation was hopeless.

The father was not a perfect parent. No one is. But he had done all he knew to do, yet his son's behavior only worsened. Finally, the man took his boy to meet with Jesus' disciples.

By this time, the father knew he desperately needed a miracle, and those were reported to be the specialty of Jesus' followers. To his dismay, the disciples declared that his son was beyond help.

At that point, the father might have given up. After all, when God's people lose hope, what else is left? But, as parents do, this dad still refused to give up on his child. He chose to disregard the negative verdicts that bombarded him, and instead he went directly to Jesus. Not surprisingly, Jesus declared that his son's situation was not hopeless. He said to the distraught dad, "If you can believe, all things are possible to him who believes." (Mark 9:23) In one of the most moving declarations in the Bible, the father cried, "Lord, I believe, help me in my unbelief!" (Mark 9:24)

The Biblical account of that poignant moment and the miracle of healing that followed is one of numerous encouraging examples found in the Scriptures that should give parents hope.[19]

19 If you'd like to read the full account, look at Matthew 17:14-21; Mark 9:14-29; Luke 9:37-42.

At some point, every parent will be in a similar position to the father in Mark's gospel. Whether it is a physical illness, a behavioral issue, a learning disability, or an emotional wound their child has been dealt, the instinctive, God-given response of a mother or father is to somehow make it better.

As a dad, I (Richard) have walked with my children through several of the setbacks I just mentioned. I would be less than honest if I didn't confess that there have been specific times when I cried out to God to deliver my child, just like the father in the passage did. And the Lord has always been faithful.

Henry Blackaby (my father) says in his book, *Experiencing God*, that you don't know the truth of your situation until you have heard from God.

Parents are inundated with platitudes and so-called wisdom, promoting methods or suggestions to ensure that their children enjoy health, success, and prosperity. Some of the conventional wisdom is good. Some of it is bad. Some of it is helpful in one context, but harmful in another. If you have reached the end of this book and concluded that Carrie and I think we have sure-fire answers, then we have not clearly communicated our hearts. As we shared in the preface, we are on an ongoing journey, just like you, to develop the best family we can. We fully intend to be successful, one day. We pray you are, too.

Finally, we want to leave you with a Scripture, a challenge, and a prayer:

God's Word says: *If you then, being evil, know how to give good gifts to your children, how much more will your Father who is in heaven give good gifts to those who ask Him! (Matthew 7:11)*

Challenge: *Never allow your previous parenting setbacks to disbearten you. Don't let your future parenting challenges daunt you. Simply strive, by God's grace, to be the finest parent you have ever been, today.*

Prayer: *Lord, thank you for these readers who have faithfully read this book through to the end. May you give them fresh resolve to tackle the challenges that lay ahead of them. May you inspire them and strengthen them to take their family to an entirely new level with you. May you guide them as they seek advice, forgiveness, and wisdom on their parenting journey. Please fill their hearts and their homes with genuine, unquenchable, contagious joy and help them make special memories with their children that continually remind them why it is so worth it to be a parent and a Christ follower. May you protect their children and help them to grow up to resemble and honor Christ. Thank you for hearing and answering our prayer. Amen.*

ABOUT THE AUTHORS

Dr. Richard Blackaby is a prolific author, international speaker, grateful husband to Lisa, and proud father to Mike, Daniel, and Carrie. He invests himself, encouraging people to seek God's best for their lives. He works with Christian business leaders, helping them to be on God's agenda in the marketplace. Richard has a Ph.D. in history and has been a life-long student of leadership. Dr. Blackaby currently serves as the president of Blackaby Ministries International (www.blackaby.org) through which he teaches business, church, and family leaders how to take their leadership to a higher level. You can keep up with him at facebook.com/ DrRichardBlackaby, twitter. com/richardblackaby and his blog at www.richardblackaby.com.

Dr. Blackaby has written numerous books including *Experiencing God, Spiritual Leadership: Moving People on to God's Agenda, God in the Marketplace: 45 Questions Fortune 500 Executives Ask About Faith, Life, and Business; The Seasons of God: How the Shifting Patterns of Your Life Reveals His Purposes for You; Unlimiting God: Increasing Your Capacity to Experience the Divine; Fresh Encounter: God's Pattern for Spiritual Awakening; Putting a Face on Grace: Living a Life Worth Passing On; Hearing God's Voice; Experiencing God: Knowing and Doing the Will of God; Called to Be God's Leader: Lessons from the Life of Joshua, Flickering Lamps; Living Out of the Overflow; Developing a Powerful Praying Church; and Spiritual Leadership Coaching.*

Carrie Blackaby is Richard Blackaby's daughter and Henry Blackaby's oldest granddaughter. She holds a BA in English, an MFA in Nonfiction Writing, and an MTS. She lives in the Atlanta area with her husband, Sam, and beautiful daughter, Claire. She works for Blackaby Ministries International.

WWW.BLACKABY.ORG

BLACKABY RESOURCES

To discover all the resources BMI offers please see
www.blackabystore.org

BLACKABY LEADERSHIP COACHING

Blackaby Ministries provides coaching-based solutions to challenges
faced by ministry and marketplace leaders. To learn more, go to
www.blackabycoaching.org

BLACKABY REVITALIZATION MINISTRY

If you sense God wants more for your church than what
you are currently experiencing, we want to help.
www.blackaby.org/revitalization

THE COLLISION

God is actively at work in the lives of the younger generation and
Blackaby Ministries is stepping out to join in this exciting activity.
www.thecollision.org

CPSIA information can be obtained
at www.ICGtesting.com
Printed in the USA
BVHW031825101121
621300BV00005B/149